IDENTIFYING CAP BADGES

A FAMILY HISTORIAN'S GUIDE

IDENTIFYING CAP BADGES

A FAMILY HISTORIAN'S GUIDE

GRAHAM BANDY

Pen & Sword
FAMILY HISTORY

First published in Great Britain in 2022 by
PEN AND SWORD FAMILY HISTORY
An imprint of
Pen & Sword Books Ltd
Yorkshire – Philadelphia

Copyright © Graham Bandy, 2022

ISBN 978 1 52677 597 9

Typeset in 10/13 Palatino by SJmagic DESIGN SERVICES, India.
Printed and bound in the UK by CPI Group (UK) Ltd, Croydon, CR0 4YY.

Pen & Sword Books Ltd incorporates the Imprints of Aviation, Atlas,
Family History, Fiction, Maritime, Military, Discovery, Politics, History,
Archaeology, Select, Wharncliffe Local History, Wharncliffe True Crime,
Military Classics, Wharncliffe Transport, Leo Cooper, The Praetorian Press,
Remember When, Seaforth Publishing and Frontline Publishing.

For a complete list of Pen & Sword titles please contact

PEN & SWORD BOOKS LTD
47 Church Street, Barnsley, South Yorkshire, S70 2AS, England
E-mail: enquiries@pen-and-sword.co.uk
Website: www.pen-and-sword.co.uk

Or
PEN & SWORD BOOKS
1950 Lawrence Rd, Havertown, PA 19083, USA
E-mail: Uspen-and-sword@casematepublishers.com
Website: www.penandswordbooks.com

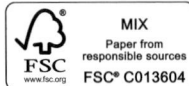

MIX
Paper from
responsible sources
FSC
www.fsc.org   FSC® C013604

CONTENTS

FOREWORD

As with so many military traditions and accoutrements, regimental and corps badges, now common in many of the world's armies, were first brought into service by the British Army. Intended to show allegiance and enable recognition among a profusion of regiments and corps on a battlefield or in a garrison town, they became the most tangible embodiment of a regiment. They were also, and remain, a symbol of the fierce pride so vital to regimental cohesion and fighting spirit. For many fighting men they hold an almost sacred place, second only to the regimental colours, and indeed some regiments' badges bear one of the battle honours emblazoned on their colours.

So significant is a soldier's badge, it often remains a part of him for the rest of his life. Sometimes literally — many men bear their regimental badge permanently tattooed on an arm or across the chest. My father, who served for only a few short years during the Second World War, displayed the three cap badges he wore on his chimney breast until the day he died when they were buried with him.

Badges have been fought over by well-fortified soldiers from rival regiments in many a garrison NAAFI and pub. They have even been used as currency in hard-bargained deals to acquire equipment and goodies from foreign allies. A resourceful soldier deploys on operations with a handful of spare badges in his pocket and I can remember many British troops gaining valuable and highly-prized American items in exchange for a humble cap badge during the Gulf War, the Balkans and Afghanistan. Beyond the battlefield, badges remain one of the most popular items among military collectors, with old and rare examples often fetching large sums.

I would be surprised if any other army, whether larger or smaller, has historically worn as wide or varied a range of badges as the British. Not only a different badge for each regiment and corps, but often different badges for different ranks within regiments and sometimes distinct badges for each battalion, perhaps differentiating regulars from reservists. All this can make accurate identification complex, but at the same time is a valuable reference point for anyone wanting to identify individual soldiers from photographs, for example those hoping to trace the military story of their forebears. For that purpose this richly-illustrated book is uniquely useful, the first such work to categorise badges according to their symbology and shape.

Himself an old soldier, Graham Bandy (with whom I served in the 2nd Battalion The Royal Anglian Regiment) possesses a profound knowledge of military badges, accoutrements and traditions. I have several times been in awe of his correction of my own erroneous identifications of regiments, time periods and locations, often through the most obscure detail. I know of many others, including experts themselves, who also turn to Graham for an authoritative answer. As he points out in the introduction, few if any books of this sort are either fully comprehensive in their listing or without error in their identification. I can say with complete confidence that you will find no such errors or omissions here. This fascinating and impressively researched volume will become an invaluable resource for all on a quest to find out about family members who served as well as those who have a fascination with the details of British military history.

Richard Kemp

PREFACE

This book is a boon to all those with a great interest in the military history of the twentieth century, but no knowledge – or interest – in regimental badges and uniforms. We so-called historians are often asked to look at a picture of some half-forgotten relative and identify the unit he was serving, sometimes even the rough date it was taken. For me the answer – without really looking as there was really no point as I don't know anything – was always, 'Sorry! No idea!' Now Graham Bandy has provided the answer. What we have needed is not some encyclopaedic tome of the millions of badges in arbitrary order of precedence of the British Army, these already exist; but to be honest you have to already know the answer before you can find it. Now we have a practical tool to swiftly and surely identify what exactly it is we are looking at – assuming that the picture is of sufficient high definition or has not been recoloured to oblivion. Graham has listed them in the old army fashion 'say what you see'. What does the badge actually show? If it looks like a lion then look under the 'Lion' chapter. Oooh look – there it is – the Herefordshire Light Infantry badge from 1947 – who would have thought it! I certainly wouldn't! This book is an invaluable 'tool of the trade' for anyone trying to identify or interpret photos. At last I will be able to help those 'curious' people who are misguided enough to think I am an expert. I will direct them to a copy of this book and all will be well! Thank you, Graham!

Peter Hart

ACKNOWLEDGEMENTS

This book has been a long haul from its conception as 'the book I always needed' through to its finale during the Covid-19 pandemic of 2020.

There are many people who have believed in me through start to finish, starting with two of my teachers, Richard and Jean Lock of Duston Upper School in Northampton (Jean was the school librarian), who said that I had at least one book in me, if not a lot more. Then some chap from the Imperial War Museum, Peter Hart (I think he has written a couple of tomes!) chivvied me along. Latterly, I met Tara from Pen and Sword at Family Tree Live! at Alexandra Palace in 2019, who saw potential in it.

Next, I must thank Toby Brayley, from the Royal Military Police Museum for the two 'Full Dress' cavalry pictures and also WO2 Vinod Shrestha for his imposing example of a Gurkha soldier in uniform (for it is he).

I must also say thank you to members of my family who dug out pictures, including those of Great Uncle Don Roberts, late ASC and the joint picture of him and 'little' Uncle Fred Attridge, late DLI and AVC.

My wife, Angela, who has supported me throughout this enterprise, and read through everything, compared and then noticed missing badges in each section. A thankless task, but on the plus side she now knows a lot more about military badges!

I must also thank fellow former Poacher, Colonel Richard Kemp and Peter Hart for their kind words, along with another fellow former Poacher and badge collector, Ian Simpson, for his help over the years.

There are many, many others whom I should mention, and if this runs to a second edition, I promise you'll be in!

Sussex Weald, August, 2020.

INTRODUCTION

The purpose of this book is to assist the family historian and those with a military interest in identifying military photographs and badges.

This is not a complete list of badges; there are other books and learned tomes on the market that list hundreds more than those that can be found here (I am yet to find a book that actually lists every badge from every single regiment without a mistake – or two – in it somewhere!).

I have purposefully left out almost all of the school and university Officer Training Corps, and the First World War Volunteer Training Corps badges. These deserve a volume to themselves. Though one or two examples have been included.

Due to family connections, I collect the badges of the Northamptonshire Regiment. From this one regiment, I have 35 variations of different regimental cap badge designs. I am still missing another 12 or so! This gives you an idea of the vast array of badges that confronts the family historian.

This book is to help identify a badge, and offer a rough timescale of use, which can lead to further research upon the person or the regiment, and a few pointers for research.

All previous books on British military badges conform to a standard ordering. They list military badges as per their units' position within the army and according to their seniority. This is known as the 'Order of Precedence'.

This can lead to confusion when trying to identify what is said to be a photo of 'Great Uncle Fred in the army', and hours can be spent pouring over learned tomes trying to match what can be seen. It is not always the case that the correct name has been attached to the photo by an aged relative. It may also be that he served in more than one regiment or corps (this was very common during the First World War). Why do the regiments have both names and numbers? What are the numbers all about?

This book can help. Instead of using the Order of Precedence, the badges are listed according to what you can see on them and their shape. If you can see a castle, search in the 'Castles' chapter for the best match, if you can see a dragon, look under the chapter headed 'Dragons'. You will then be able to match what you have with a badge and regiment quickly and easily. The badges have also been helpfully cross-referenced, so if there is a star *and* a cross visible, the badge can be found in both the 'Cross' chapter *and* the 'Star' chapter.

ORDER OF PRECEDENCE

The Order of Precedence is explained thus: when a unit or regiment of the British Army 'forms up' on parade with other units, their placement on the parade, whether front or rear of a marching body, or left to right on a parade ground, depends upon a number of factors. These include the length of their service to the crown, when they were formed and with which regiments they were amalgamated. These things dictate the unit's position and seniority in the army. This is called the Order of Precedence, and those on the right of the parade, or at the front of the marching body are the most senior. As you get further down the parade, the more junior the units become.

The only exception to the rule is when the Royal Horse Artillery parade with their cannon. They then form up on the extreme right of the parade. This dates back to 1794 when a British battery distinguished itself so well at the battle of Vaux that the Duke of York ordered that the entire allied contingent of troops march past them. Now when the King's Troop forms up on parade with other units, they take up the 'honourable position' to the right.

I have listed some Orders of Precedence from different times to illustrate the many disbandments, amalgamations and changes of names that have happened over the years. These can be found later on in the book.

The last amalgamations for cavalry units (at the time of writing) took place in 2015 upon the formation of the Royal Lancers, and in 2007 for the infantry when the 'Mercian Regiment' and 'The Rifles' were created.

Cavalry and infantry regiments were named after their colonels upon formation. Prince Rupert's Horse and Waller's Horse were on opposing sides during the War of the Three Kingdoms (the Civil War), and when it came for the infantry to be named they were also named after the chap who raised them. This could cause long and difficult names, for example, Colonel Cholmondeley's Regiment of Foot (formed 1741), followed by more problems when the founding colonel died or a new one was appointed. Eventually it was deemed necessary to number the regiments, and so, from 1751, they were numbered from 1 to 109 and then given a title, such as His Majesty's 1st Regiment of Foot (The Royal Scots).

The cavalry was also given numbers, related as to when they were formed, and the length of time in service to the crown.

Later, the infantry regiments were assigned to counties, and in 1881 the first of the big reorganisations of the army occurred. Many know the film *Zulu* and the heroic defence of Rorke's Drift in 1879 that it portrayed. What most don't know is that it wasn't until 1881 that the South Wales Borderers were formed and, as at Isandlwana, the regiment concerned was the 24th (2nd Warwickshire) Regiment of Foot. They weren't actually 'Welsh' until two years after the battle.

Up until 1881, these numbers could be seen on cap badges. After this date they were perpetuated in the regimental titles, crests and a number of other official and unofficial items.

The last of these, the 22nd (Cheshire) Regiment, only lost its singular order of precedence numbering in 2006 when it became the 1st Battalion of the Mercian Regiment.

This 'reform' and the many subsequent reforms and amalgamations have caused great confusion amongst casual military readers and family historians. One of the biggest was in 1959 when all infantry regiments were made part of a brigade. This 'Brigade System' did not last long but badges were produced. I have included a selection of these.

Another matter of confusion is the re-establishment of the Home Guard in the early 1950s. This only lasted from 1951-1957. Again, a selection of badges is included.

As the new badges are within living memory and easily researched, I have mainly stuck to the pre-1964 regiments, but I have included some after this date for illustrative purposes.

A SHORT HISTORY OF THE BADGE IN THE BRITISH ARMY

The regimental devices worn by the British Army predate the existence of a standing professional army.

When the followers or serfs tied to a nobleman or landowner were mustered, they wore the badge of their liege as a distinguishing mark so they could tell friend from foe in the fog of battle.

Badges were well known during the Cousins' Wars (Wars of the Roses), where 'the Cat, the Rat and Lovell the dog, Rule all England under a Hog.' This verse was posted on St Paul's Cathedral in 1484 and refers to King Richard III (the hog, whose badge was a white boar) and his leading counsellors, William Catesby (the cat), Sir Richard Ratcliffe (the rat) and Francis, Viscount Lovell (the dog – his heraldic crest featured a wolf). Emblems were well enough known for people to understand to whom they referred.

Likewise, at the same time, the Bear and Ragged Staff of Warwick the Kingmaker was also well known. This device continued to be used by the Royal Warwickshire Regiment on the collar and also by the Warwickshire Yeomanry.

The Yorkist White Rose appeared upon the East Yorkshire Regiment and the King's Own Yorkshire Light Infantry until amalgamation, as did the East Lancashire and Loyal North Lancashires with the Red Rose of Lancaster.

The rose on the Hampshire Regiment's badge comes from the gift given to Winchester by Henry V on his journey to the coast and, ultimately, Agincourt.

Except for the guards and some of the more venerable line infantry who were awarded royal devices, most regiments, until the mid-18th century, wore the livery and devices of their founders. In 1751, George II ordered the end of the personal devices of colonels, as well as ordering the sequential numbering of the regiments.

The British Army, its arms, services, and various affiliated units have all been proud of their badges, so much so that when a soldier collected badges of other units on his belt, it became known as a 'Hate Belt'. There are stories and even poems of soldiers from different regiments fighting with each other since time immemorial; that is when they are not fighting the enemy!

Over the years, various units have sprung up alongside the regular standing army. Although the Royal Navy can trace its ancestry back to the time of King Alfred, there was no actual standing army until the New Model Army of the Commonwealth was formed by Oliver Cromwell in 1645. This was stood down at the Restoration of King Charles II and then reformed. The Coldstream Guards laid down their weapons and were then ordered to pick them up again as soldiers of the King.

Since then, at times of emergency, various volunteer units have been formed. For many years, the militia was always in the background. In fact there was a county lottery in which men were randomly chosen to serve. These, as time progressed (in 1881 under the far reaching Cardwell Reforms), became the volunteer battalions of the various infantry regiments. The cavalry had their own equivalent, the yeomanry, which basically consisted of volunteers on horseback. These date back even further to when gentlemen rode their horses to defend their county or their lord.

These yeomanry regiments were originally formed in response to French aggression in 1794. The then Prime Minister, Pitt the Younger, suggested a force of volunteer yeoman cavalry should be formed to defend the nation against invasion and to subdue insurrection in the counties if called upon. In February 1797, a French force of four ships carrying the 'Legion Noir' was sighted off Carregwasted Point in Pembrokeshire. This was part of a three-way attack on Britain by the French. The Pembroke Yeomanry and the Pembroke Militia were mustered under Lord Cawdor and eventually, after the ships had left and the French (American) commander saw no other way out, the force surrendered to him. It is an interesting tale and worth reading up on.

In 1853, Her Majesty Queen Victoria granted the battle honour, 'Fishguard', to the Pembroke Yeomanry. Their descendants are now the only unit in the British Army to carry a battle honour won on British soil and were the first volunteer unit to receive one. Incidentally, the French 'invasion' was the last time troops in numbers made an attempted land invasion of Great Britain.

The descendant unit is 22 (Pembrokeshire Yeomanry) Transport Squadron, part of 157 (Welsh Regt) RLC (Reserve).

Added to these were the Victorian Rifle Volunteer Units, who were affiliated to the county regiments, but wore grey uniforms and Light

Infantry type badges. These were raised in the mid-19th century; again, as a response to French aggression.

These were all part-time 'home only' soldiers who paraded once a week and went to a training camp at weekends. They did not serve overseas until 1900 when volunteers were taken to the Second Boer War in South Africa.

In 1908, another reorganisation joined all these disparate 'weekend warrior' units under a blanket organisation, the 'Territorial Force'. After the First World War, this became the 'Territorial Army', then the 'Territorial Army and Volunteer Reserve' and, more recently, 'The Reserves'.

These units had a wide array of cap and collar badges, a large number of which can be found in this volume.

Be aware that when researching a photograph of a pre-First World War soldier, he may not be a regular, and thus his records are scant and more difficult to find. One in three records of the rank and file from the First World War survive. The remainder were burnt in an incendiary attack on London in November 1940.

Closer inspection of a badge will reveal many things and a long history. Battle honours, much like the wreaths and ribbons awarded to a Roman legion after a successful battle and carried on their eagle, were similar to the battle honours on the colours carried by a British Army unit. These colours carried the names of battles where the distinguished fighting of that unit had been recognised and classed as a 'battle honour'. These honours were frequently transferred to the badges.

The main proponent of this was the 17th Lancers. The colonel of their antecedent regiment, the 17th Light Dragoons, brought the news of Wolfe's victory at Quebec (in 1759, during the Seven Years' War) to George II. Wolfe had been mortally wounded just as the battle was won and the King ordered that the regiment wear a skull and crossbones badge with the motto 'Or Glory' to commemorate this. At the time it was believed that these were the only parts of the body required for the resurrection on Judgement Day.

The Scots Greys, the Royal Irish Fusiliers and the Essex Regiment had a French eagle on their badges. These had been captured by the regiments during the Napoleonic wars.

Many badges have a horn or bugle horn within the design. These denote regiments that were in the light infantry role. The Somerset Light Infantry (13th Foot) has a mural crown above, surmounting the horn, with a scroll saying 'Jellalabad' upon it. This commemorates the regiment holding the earthquake damaged walls of the town against a long siege. This also gave them the title 'The Illustrious Garrison'.

The Gloucestershire Regiment (28th Foot) had a unique honour in that they wore a badge on the back of their hats as well as the front. At the battle of Alexandria in 1801 they were hard pressed and surrounded. The order came, 'rear rank, right about face, fire!', and they stood back to back with their comrades. Thus standing, they eventually repulsed the attack by the French, successfully forcing them back into the town of Alexandria to surrender. The back badge tradition is continued by the successor regiment, The Rifles, the 1st Battalion of which contains the old Glosters.

Another successful siege is remembered in the badges of the four Gibraltar regiments. The Great Siege of Gibraltar was from 24 June 1779 to 7 February 1783. Spain had entered the war on the side of the French and revolting American colonists, and their proximity and spurious claims made the 'gateway to the Mediterranean' vulnerable. The castle and key to Gibraltar, along with the motto, 'Montis Insignia Calpe', was incorporated into the regimental devices. These regiments are Suffolk, Essex, Northamptonshire and Dorset.

At the battle of Almanza in 1707, during the reign of Queen Anne, what became the Norfolk Regiment successfully covered Lord Galway's retreat. From a total of 467 officers and men, 324 were lost. For this gallant action, the device of Britannia was awarded. Later on when fighting the Spanish, the Britannia device was mistaken for an image of the Virgin Mary, and hence the nickname of 'The Holy Boys' was born.

Tigers are seen on a number of badges including the Leicestershire's and the Hampshire's, and latterly as the name of the Princess of Wales' Royal Regiment, known as the Tigers, but referred to as the 'Squidgies' by other members of the army. This is in response to a taped telephone call between Princess Diana of Wales and James Gilby where he referred to her as 'Squidgy'. The tiger emblem itself refers to long service in India.

The Royal Scots Greys and the Queen's Bays names referred to the colour of the horses used by each regiment.

The Queen's Royal West Surrey Regiment (2nd Foot), who were raised in 1661 by the Earl of Peterborough, were known as 'Kirke's Lambs' from 1682 because of the badge and its then colonel. They received the Paschal Lamb device from the House of Braganza when it was formed to garrison Tangier. The regimental march is also called 'Braganza'.

Due to the many amalgamations and disbandments, a number of these stories and even the devices have marched off into the sunset. That being said, many of the regimental battle honours are still remembered today in the successor regiments. The 2nd Battalion, The Royal Anglian Regiment, for example, features a castle from the Suffolk, Essex and Northamptonshire Regiments on its cap badge, the sphynx of Egypt and a scroll with Talavera on its collar badges from the Royal Lincolnshire and Northamptonshire, and, on the soldiers' arms, the eagle captured by the Essex Regiment during the Peninsular War from the French. Talavera, Sobroan and Minden day are all still celebrated today.

HOW TO USE THIS BOOK

This book is, as mentioned, set out in a way that you can look for the shape of the badge, rather than a name you have no idea of.

First, look for what you can see. Does it have a crown on top of it? Can you see wings, or something else?

The contents page lists the badges by feature in their chapters so once you've identified one of the prominent features, use the contents list to find the right section. Please note that if you see more than one thing, it will be listed under that section too, so you can easily cross-reference.

Sadly, some photos you may find are either too poor in quality or they have been played around with, so you can't see anything much at all. The modern culprits for this are photocopies of originals and, sadly, poor restorations of photos by misguided amateurs who don't have the facilities Peter Jackson did when he made his First World War film in colour a couple of years ago. Pixelation is totally lost by the smudging process, and 99 times out of 100, the amateur colouring-in enthusiast doesn't research what the colours of the uniforms actually are. Thus you end up with something that is neither accurate nor legible anymore. This could well be handed down to subsequent generations as 'how it was' when it wasn't.

Always, always look at an original photo if possible. If that isn't available, ask the relative for a high resolution scan. Some of these old photos are so good, you can often make out what is actually on the buttons. The late Victorian/early Edwardian 'cabinet' photos are very good for this.

As always, the devil is in the detail, and the more detail you can see, the better. It is also best practice to have a scanner or a magnifying glass available alongside this book and the original photo – or a high resolution scan of it!

Chapter 1

UNIFORMS AND BADGES IN DATE ORDER AND SOME TIPS TO HELP WITH DATING

Dating with Crowns

There are four basic types of crown on a badge, they are as follows:

The Queen Victoria crown (I am using the vernacular, beloved by collectors, in order to place them on a timeline) was in use up until the Queen died in 1901. It can been seen on quite a few badges here.

The King's crown, which covers Edward VII, George V, Edward VIII and George VI was in use from 1902 until 1952. On some badges the Royal Monogram is visible, so this also helps date a badge to a particular monarch's reign.

Queen Victoria's Crown, up to 1901   *King's Crown, from 1902 to 1952*

Queen Elizabeth Crown, 1953 to date   *Of course, there are also other types of crown*

The Queen Elizabeth crown has featured on military badges since 1953.

Sadly there are a number of ducal crowns, coronets, etc that do not fit into these categories, but, basically, this is the yardstick by which one can start working out the dates.

I have used the same badge above for reference. Although technically not a cap badge, it has been used thus on several occasions. It is much easier to see the differences when the badge is the same.

Oddly, the Northamptonshire Regiment, whose collar badges are seen here, was never granted the prefix 'Royal' during its lifetime, nor did it have a crown on its main cap badge. It wasn't until it became the '2nd (Duchess of Gloucester's Own Royal Lincolnshire and Northamptonshire) Battalion The East (later Royal) Anglian Regiment' that it gained the honour. Incidentally, when the new battalion was created, it also created the longest ever official name in the British Army.

The Home Service Helmet Plate with the crown variations (which can be seen on page 36), was universal for all infantry regiments. Only the centre of the plate differed. Likewise the variations on the Shako plate, the only variations up until 1881 were the centres of each badge. After the reforms of 1881, the affiliated county name and a device is prominent.

Uniform photographs, in date order

Pictures of soldiers survive from the early days of photography. This is often problematic due to the vast array of Victorian uniforms, which changed greatly throughout the period. I will not go into great detail here as uniforms are a book unto themselves! The above pictures show officers in the 1860s or 1870s. Their regiment is easy to identify as they have numbers on their hats. Officers also wore a particular type of uniform.

There were several badges in this period which will be discussed later, but here is an easy one to begin with. The 48 on the officer's pattern cap on the previous page shows that they are members of the 48th of Foot.

In 1881 they were joined with the 58th to become the 1st and 2nd Battalions of the Northamptonshire Regiment. All line infantry regiments of this period in this dress will show the number. This number can be checked with the list on page 287.

The Victorian picture to the left shows an officer of the Northamptonshire Yeomanry which the Tudor Rose of the county and the collar badges confirm. Photos of this era have the most marvellous resolution, and sometimes even the name of the unit on the buttons can be read with a magnifying glass!

It is also interesting to note the photographer, as this can sometimes help ascertaining the unit's location at the time the photo was taken. This can also help confirm the identity or battalion of the unit, as lists of postings are available. As yeomanry, this soldier was only part time, much like the Territorial Army, militia and the Reserve of today.

A soldier in a scarlet tunic or frock is shown to the bottom left. The Glengarry hat (often mistaken for Scottish regiments only) was approved for use by all line infantry regiments in 1874, and special 'Glengarry Badges' were approved. These can be seen on page 34. The 7 button 'Home Service Frock' is pictured with what are known as 'jam pot cuffs', so named as they resemble the old style of white ceramic jam pots of the period. This dates the picture prior to 1902. Combined with the Glengarry we have a date of between 1874 and the mid-1890s when the Field Service Cap was rolled out as an issue item.

On the right we have another Victorian officer, note the elaborate cuffs and embroidery on the uniform. This cuff embroidery and the single crown on his shoulder boards denote a major. The collar badges around his neck show a grenade. This could be a number of regiments and corps. What singles this chap out though is cuff lace and the visibility of a field gun on his buttons. Yes, these 'cabinet cards' can really have this amount of detail.

The field gun and the other accoutrements show that this chap is a major in the Royal Artillery, but there is more! He has a medal which is so very clear on the original and, of course, even better under a magnifying glass. It is the Victorian era Volunteer Decoration, which gave recipients the (rather unfortunate) post nominal letters, VD. This was later altered after the 1908 reforms and it became the Territorial Decoration (TD). He is a part-time soldier, and this is the item that marks him out as such on this picture. So, here is a major of the Volunteer Royal Artillery of the 1880s to 1890s with the VD.

The picture below is easier to date. It has 1895 on the original and shows the Mounted Infantry of the 1st Battalion Northamptonshire Regiment in Bangalore or Secunderbad as they marched off to the latter location in October 1895.

Snippets from this photo are used throughout this chapter as 1895 was a time of transition and many variations can be seen in one place. For example there are four or five different types of jacket, and two different types of hat with two different types of cap badge!

What can be seen here is the Khaki Drill uniform worn in the warmer climes of the world. As a yardstick, one can say that this type and colour of tunic (with or without similar coloured trousers) would be worn in all posts east (and south) of Gibraltar except sometimes during the cooler winter months. It is made of a lightweight cotton material, and is much better for work in such climes than the scarlet tunics seen everywhere up to the late 1880s.

On the left is my grandfather, George Bandy of the 6th Dragoon Guards, in 1897. He had joined one year earlier and would go on to serve in the Second Boer War and in the Home Guard during the Second World War. I have found no record of him in the First World War as yet. Sadly his medals are missing and, as my first cousins are all 40-50 or so years older than me, there are no clues as to where they are. Lost family medals happens to all of us.

What you can see is the uniform of 'Dragoons of the Line' with the plumed helmet and sword. He was a private soldier – not an officer – and yet still carried a sword as he was cavalry. The large number 6 in the centre of the helmet star can be seen quite well on the original photograph.

On the next page you can see two more dress uniforms of the period, Hussars and Lancers, which are often mistaken for the uniforms of other countries.

Above we have the 9th Lancers at Canterbury. Notice the 'Czapka' helmet that marks them out as Lancers, and they can also been seen carrying their lances.

To the right, we see a sergeant of the 11th Hussars, who were known as the 'Cherrypickers' due to their cherry-coloured trousers and their picking of cherries in an orchard before a battle. The hussars jackets are very similar in a number of regiments, and it can be very difficult to ascertain the tiny details that mark them apart. Luckily for us, senior non-commissioned officers, such as this sergeant, wear a badge above their chevrons. This is quite patently the tall badge of the 11th and, coupled with all the other details, we can see he is a hussar from this regiment and it is circa 1890.

The Other Ranks Walking Out Dress (below, right), worn from 1902 until August 1914, when scarlets were withdrawn from most of the army. This is easy to date as he has pointed cuffs. He carries a Walking Out Cane (not a photographer's prop, as can often be misconstrued) and the new 1902 pattern peaked cap.

The sergeant major of a Northamptonshire Rifle Volunteer battalion, pre-1908 but post-

1902 because of the cap badge and grey uniform he is wearing. He also still wears the Rifles cross belt which disappeared after 1908 (top left).

Top right is an officer wearing the 1902 pattern Frock Coat, which differed from its forebears by not having flaps all the way down the front. It is also noteworthy that he has a Wolseley Helmet, for Full Dress in warmer climes, complete with spike. As you can see on the front, the badge is very clear.

Continuing the theme of Rifle Volunteers and Volunteer battalions, on the bottom of the opposite page we have two from about the same time; 1904 to 1908. On the left is a cornet player of the Kettering Volunteer Rifles Band, wearing a grey uniform with a fur cap. On the right is not an Australian but a member of the 1st Volunteer Battalion of the Northamptonshire Regiment. From about 1899 to 1908 the slouch hat was worn by many members of the British Army, not only in the warmer climes of South Africa, but also at home as can be seen in this picture and the image below.

Right: The Brodrick Cap, loved by few, loathed by many. An imitation of the German 'pork pie' hat, it was introduced in 1903 and worn officially until around 1907. I have pictures of them still in use in late 1908 in India. Named after the secretary of state for war, most people despised them. They were (allegedly) laughed at by young ladies, jeered at by youths, and in one unfortunate case, said to have caused the suicide of a soldier, who could no longer stand the shame of wearing such a headdress.

In 1907 the Service Dress Cap (Other Ranks) was introduced, and soldiers were spared the humiliation of this now very rare piece of uniform.

The Brodrick is worn in the bottom image on page 9 by two members of the Northamptonshire Regiment. The pre-First World War cloth shoulder titles can also be seen, as well as the detachable shoulder boards. This uniform, the Other Ranks Service Dress, was issued from 1902, and was worn for almost the next 60 years in one iteration or another.

The bandolier is the 1899 pattern, seen on many Second Boer War pictures.

The transition from the Brodrick cap shown on the 1st Battalion of the Northamptonshire Regiment in India in 1908.

The 1907 Service Dress Cap (Other Ranks) and the Imperial Service Badge

A private of the Royal Army Medical Corps is shown opposite (middle right). He is a trained medical orderly, which is denoted by the Geneva Cross arm badges. They were not called medics at this time, that term arrived in the British Army many decades later. The stiff crown of the SD cap indicates pre-1916 when the internal wire was removed. He is wearing the 1907 Service Dress Tunic with stitched plain epaulettes, not the detachable or twisted cord earlier incarnations from 1902 onwards (the detachable version are seen on the previous page). The straight line shoulder title reads RAMC.

The badge over his right breast pocket is the Imperial Service badge. During the Second Boer War, many yeomanry and volunteer battalions went out to South Africa to bolster the regular forces out there. After the formation of the Territorial Force in 1908, their duties only included those within (and in defence of) the British Isles. In 1910 the County Associations, which administered the territorials, sent out the 'Imperial Service Declaration' forms where individuals could attest that they were willing to serve overseas if the need arose. After signing they were given this badge. Territorial Force units took great pride in the amount of service men (and women) who had signed up thus.

Below: Two pictures taken from a larger photo of a Lincolnshire Regiment Volunteer Band. The officer on the left is wearing the pre-1912 officer's Service Dress Tunic with Sam Browne belt, and leather

'Stowasser' leggings. The trombonist is a corporal, and has three proficiency stars on his lower right arm, along with a 'lozenge' for current years proficiency. The badge above his chevrons is the old style musician/ bandsman trade badge featuring two crossed trumpets. This could be post 1908 and the formation of the Territorial Force, or it may be a bit earlier, as the corporal is wearing the 1907 pattern Other Ranks Service Dress hat. Sadly it is not dated, but would be in the area of 1907 to 1914.

At the time of the First World War, many of those who were volunteering for the Empire and Dominion forces were first or second generation immigrants. They were still very patriotic towards Great Britain, and some even came home to sign up. That notwithstanding, those who did sign up in their new homes still had photos sent back to the old country, and these frequently turn up in family collections. The uniforms are almost like British ones but have differences. Below left is a Canadian 7 button tunic, which is easily identifiable by the sheer amount and size of the buttons. British tunics had 5. The collar is a bit different, as are the pocket flaps. The Australian tunic was belted and, also, just that bit different. Whilst there were many badges associated with these forces, the most obvious and, indeed, frequent ones, are shown right.

The Canadian maple leaf to the top and the Australian 'Rising Sun' badge, lower. Australians at this time mainly wore the slouch hats but beware, as per the earlier pictures in this section!

By the end of the war, the Canadian tunic had all but disappeared amongst the other ranks (and sometimes the officers in the front line), as all were wearing the British version, which makes identification just that little bit more difficult.

Unlike the British records, the Australian and Canadian ones are fully extant, and free to access.

Below is a picture showing two soldiers who are often mistaken for postmen or similar. It is in fact what became known as 'Blue Emergency Clothing' or 'Kitchener's Blues'. A simple jacket and trousers issued to the vast numbers of men who had volunteered following Kitchener's call for new armies after the outbreak of war. These can be seen on the various Pals battalions that the army encouraged ('Join together, train together, fight together'). Stocks of uniforms were not available in the numbers required and so the men paraded, initially, in civilian clothes.

Gradually the blue uniforms appeared as a 'stop gap' and all sorts of hats and badges can be seen being worn with them in various photographs. Here we have 1890s Field Service Caps dug out of some forgotten stores and issued. Many wore shoulder titles as badges, either on the hats or on the collars, and lots of obsolete items were issued. It's difficult to clothe a unit when 1,088 men appear over two days for just one battalion! It took from the beginning of September until the beginning of October 1914 for the blue emergency uniform to be issued and the first khaki uniforms were issued to these volunteers in January 1915. Thus there was a short window for these blue uniforms from October 1914 to January 1915.

The khaki uniforms were mostly of the simplified type, without pocket pleats and shoulder pads. This is the so called 1915 tunic (by modern collectors). This Tunic, Simplified was, in fact, approved in late 1914, due to restrictions in cloth supply and the enormous amount of volunteers turning up to join. In

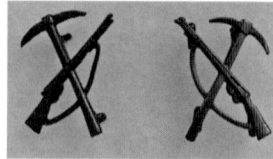

1916 the supply situation had evened out and the patches and pleats were reinstated. So even these tunics had a short lifespan.

The above soldier, from the Royal Sussex Regiment (Cinque Ports Batallion), is also wearing collar badges. This identifies him as being with a pioneer battalion. All infantry pioneer battalions in the First World War wore these: a crossed rifle and pick axe. Thus, any soldier or officer wearing these can be pinned down to a particular battalion of the regiment featured on the cap badge. In this soldier's case, it confirms that he is in

the 5th Cinque Ports Battalion of the Royal Sussex Regiment. The 1914 belt also helps as it was initially issued to the Kitchener volunteer battalions, of which the above was a member. He wears the Tunic, Simplified (see page 13).

'Service Battalions' were formed from the Kitchener 1 (or K1) volunteers. The local volunteers were assigned to county regiments, and then given the next battalion numbers available for that regiment. Hence the first Kitchener battalion in the Northamptonshire Regiment was the 5th Service, next came the 6th Service and then the 7th Service Battalion. (The 1st and 2nd battalions of

Boer War veteran

the regiment were the regulars, the 3rd was the old Militia Battalion and the 4th Battalion was the Territorial Battalion.) Therefore one service battalion from the K1 was allocated Pioneers, and in the Northamptonshire Regiment it was the 5th Battalion, and in the case of the Royal Sussex, the 8th. This rule applied to all infantry regiments.

Just to add some grist to the mill as per the 'Kitchener Blues' on page 13. On the left is a Second Boer War veteran who has re-joined the Northamptonshire Regiment and has been issued a collar badge to use as a cap badge, just the same as the 1895 picture earlier on. There are always exceptions that prove the rule, of course, and here is one!

The Royal Flying Corps was formed in April 1912, and the Royal Naval Air Service a year later. Pictured above right is a lance corporal air mechanic in his 'maternity' jacket. This had no outside buttons that could snag in machinery, and was specific to the RFC. An officer's version was also worn. There was great rivalry in the procurement of aeroplanes between the RFC and the RNAS, which hindered their effectiveness in the First World War. In 1917, General Jan Christian Smuts, a former Boer War Commando who was now a politician and General in the South African Forces, presented a paper to the British government, stating that any future war would be an air war, destroying civilian industrial and military targets on an enormous scale, and that there should be an Air Force on a par with the Navy and Army to counteract this. This was well received and a year later the RAF was formed.

The Royal Air Force was formed on 1 April 1918 (a source of great mirth to the Army and Royal Navy) and the uniforms of the RNAS and RFC were worn for quite some time after April 1918, especially for the officers and pilots; although the Other Airman's (Other Airmen is the same as the army's Other Ranks) new RAF uniforms came early. The image to the right shows one from 1919 until the 1930s. The badge – with the crown change – has remained the same through to present day.

One military badge that can be seen on civilian clothing towards the end of the First World War and for many years after is the 'Silver War Badge.' This was awarded to honourably discharged personnel from all services, and also the Empire and Dominions (on the left). It was given to the sick or injured to show they had done their bit and could not be subjected to the women who stalked the omnibus routes and streets handing out white feathers to those whom they judged to be cowards as they were not in uniform.

First awarded in 1916, it was also given retrospectively, so those discharged earlier in the war received one too. Some 1,150,000 were bestowed, and most of the personnel were also awarded pensions. The badges all have individual numbers which correspond to an entry on the SWB roll and is indicated on the Medal Index Cards. These numbers are neither regimental nor service numbers.

Below you can see two men in a different uniform. These are convalescing personnel who have been injured or sick. Many would return to full service but a number were discharged after a medical board showed they were no longer fit for military service. They are wearing 'Hospital Blues'

of the early war pattern, with white open jacket collars, white shirts and red ties. They were usually worn with the service cap of the individual.

On the right is the second or later type of Hospital Blues seen during, and indeed after, the First World War. Here it is shown with the Service Dress Cap. No gentleman of any rank would wear headdress inside a building, so here we are outside. He is, again, a Northamptonshire.

Note the lack of white collars on the jacket. These were of a much lighter blue than the original issue. Hospital Blues were also only worn at major base hospitals (e.g. Etaples in France and Alexandria in Egypt) or the war hospitals and convalescent hospitals back in Britain. These were scattered all over the country and contained anywhere between 6 and 1,000 beds. They could be anything from a converted golf clubhouse to a stately home or even a converted county lunatic asylum.

To give some idea of the extent of these facilities, let's look at Northamptonshire, a typical rural county. Within this county there were almost 40 of these establishments which treated 23,000 patients. If you extrapolate this across the country, you can see the amount of beds available for the evacuated cases – this does not count those treated in France and Flanders that did not get a 'Blighty one', i.e. a wound that sent them home.

An interesting fact in reference to these uniforms: soldiers were not allowed to consume alcohol whilst convalescing. In fact, one landlady and her barmaid were fined £60 each for serving beer to a wounded soldier in Hospital Blues (this equates to almost £5,400 in 2020). They were allowed 'hospital leave', but not to drink, as it interfered with treatment.

Post-1918, uniforms and badges changed little for a while. The army went on to fight the Bolsheviks in Northern Russia, occupy Germany and, later, Turkey. Parts of the Empire began to stir and mumble malcontent and the Empire and Dominions had seen the unifying effects of the war and an increased ideation of 'self' as opposed to binding to Great Britain. After the Easter Rising in 1916 in Ireland, the pre-war Home Rule followers lost out to a civil war, which changed the face of the army as the 5 Irish regiments most associated with what was now the new Irish Free State in the south of Ireland were disbanded, and a number of cavalry regiments were lost to amalgamations too.

Pictured on the bottom of page 17 is a gunner of the Royal Artillery. The three former sections (Royal Horse, Royal Field and Royal Garrison Artillery) had been amalgamated into one homogenous unit.

In 1921 new ideas on uniform were implemented.

To the left we can see what is often identified as the '1922 pattern' uniform (totally erroneously as there was never such a thing). It was approved in 1921 and began issue thereafter. Collar badges have appeared universally on Service Dress for Other Ranks, and the peak of the Service Dress Cap has grown into some huge edifice. What is also apparent on this uniform is the better cut and fit, and the loss of one visible seam from the collar to the shoulder pads. The earlier version had two quite patent ones but here we have just the one. This, coupled with the ginormous peak and the collar badges, identify this as a post-First World War uniform. This uniform stayed in the army until the 1960s surprisingly enough. It is quite easy to see the differences, but many people are unaware and think any pictures in Service Dress are from the First World War, when they can actually be from anywhere between 1902 and 1960.

The 'East Of Gibraltar' Khaki Drill uniform began to change too, although, as stated earlier, things took time to filter out into the Empire. The chap pictured opposite (top) has his Wolseley Helmet (introduced in 1900) on the table. He is wearing a tunic that would not be out of place during the First World War, but the badge pictured was not authorised until 1919, when the Army Ordnance Corps was granted the prefix,

Royal. It could really be any time from 1919 to the late 1920s, but this narrows the time frame slightly for the family researcher. Around this date the pocket flaps became straight and not pointed as we see here.

A number of people would look at the picture below and simply think, Royal Artillery or, more popularly, Royal Field Artillery. Why? you may ask. The gentleman pictured here has spurs, mounted puttees, a 1903 bandolier and a white lanyard but 'only the Royal Artillery had white lanyards' some might say. Well, this image of a member of the military transport platoon of the Northamptonshire Regiment puts that assumption to bed. The world and his wife wore white lanyards, especially during the First World War, as the issue pocket knife was attached to them. The army was slowly mechanising but horses were used by every arm and branch of the army, so every arm, branch and unit needed people to work with horses. All you can confidently say about most pictures featuring

this 'look' is that the gentleman worked with horses; doubly so if the cap badge is not visible!

The white lanyard was adopted by the Royal Artillery in the 1920s and the scurrilous rumour went around – and still does – that the white lanyard was for cowardice as the guns were abandoned. The guns of the Royal Artillery being their colours, this was a most pernicious rumour. Of course, interservice and interunit rivalry has not changed since the first time a drunken soldier from the Roman Army's 12th Legion insulted a soldier of the 9th Legion and made jokes about him disappearing into the mists, never to be seen again. The 9th Legion vanished from the history books and lost its eagle (colours) whilst on a punitive expedition 'north of the wall' into Caledonia. Of course, if a group of plebeians were to make the same joke, the two legionaries would join forces and take them all on. As our two legionaries might say *Omnia mutantur, nihil interi* (Everything changes (but), nothing perishes). Above we have another Northamptonshire soldier of the 1930s, in Walking Out Dress as per the previous page, with another ginormous peak! This time a white dress belt is used.

Something a little different as we move forward to 1937. On the bottom of the opposite page we see a group of women from the Queen Alexandra's Imperial Military Nursing Service (QAIMNS), gathered at Southampton to make history. These sisters are in the rather unfamiliar 'Walking Out Dress' of the QAIMNS. Badges (see page 246) can be seen on both the collars of the greatcoat and the Norfolk jacket (far right).

These nursing sisters are being flown to Gibraltar, on a flying boat from Southampton, to tend to wounded German sailors from the *Deutschland* after two Spanish Republican aircraft mistook the ship for the Spanish Nationalist *Canaris*.

31 German sailors were killed and 74 wounded, the most serious of whom were taken ashore at Gibraltar. The ship was anchored off Ibiza as part of the International Non-Intervention Committee Patrol – supposedly a blockade against ships taking supplies to either the Republican or Nationalist sides in the Spanish Civil War. The next day the German Heavy Cruiser *Admiral Scheer* shelled the city of Almeria, killing 19 and wounding 55 in retaliation.

The Army Nursing Services were formalised in 1881, and from this time nurses were part of the chain of command. The QAIMNS were formed in 1902 after the Second Boer War from 'lessons learned'. The Reserve (QAIMNS R) was formed in 1908, along with the Territorial Force Nursing Service. This, in turn, became the Territorial Army Nursing Service in 1920, and all three were gathered together under the new name, Queen Alexandra's Royal Army Nursing Corps, in 1949. In 1992 male nurses were admitted to the Corps for the first time.

RAF uniforms of 1937 (below). These airmen are helping the QAIMNS nurses seen on the previous page aboard the flying boat. This has been the basic look since 1919, but on the cusp of the Second World War these

'Other Airman's' uniforms gained an open jacket with collar and tie, as can be seen in the picture overleaf.

Interestingly, the chaps centre front and right rear on the image overleaf are wearing 'Battledress', the khaki coloured uniform usually seen on members of the army, and very rarely at this date on anything other than the RAF Regiment. These two

airmen are from Number 31 Mobile Field Hospital in Carthage, North Africa, in March 1944. One would expect RAF 'War Service Dress' but these are American-made 'War Aid' battledress. Other Airman's RAF uniforms are usually very easy to spot because of the eagle insignia at the top of the arm, which can be seen clearly in both pictures.

At first glance, these two Royal Marines (below) look as if they could be from the First World War, but they are not.

The chap on the left is in Patrol Dress (later known as No1s in the army) and wears a 1908 pattern belt, as seen in the First World War. The chap on the right is still in Service Dress, but carries a more modern respirator haversack than those found in the First World War. The huge peak of the cap (again) on the right indicates later as well. This is either very late 1930s or even 1940. Pictures of the Dunkirk evacuation show a number of troops in this dress. The cap badge is quite clear as the globe and laurel of the Royal Marines. At this date they were stationed on land as well as ships, but were not yet commandos.

Home Guard uniforms from 1941 (opposite left) and 1943 (opposite right). What singles them out as Home Guard is, as usual, in the detail. The lad on the left has a Home Guard brassard on his right arm, and the Home Guard peculiarity, leather anklets. These can also be seen in the

photo on the right. The regular army wore 'Anklets, Web' (not Gaitors or Gaiters). Also note the white undershirt of the lad on the left.

The cap badges were of the County Line Infantry Regiment, and the shoulder titles included a county designation patch and a battalion number.

The Home Guard was initially formed as the Local Defence Volunteers in 1940 to provide a local militia with local knowledge to assist the forces should the invasion come. They soon became more allied to the army hierarchy and then mirrored them.

Although those under 18 years old were admitted, it was not uncommon for 15 and 16 year olds to be found. As time went on and equipment became available, they were turned into a formidable fighting force with an array of interesting and useful weaponry.

It was not a joke unit with old duffers doing silly things as perception has it now, but a force of fully trained soldiers, most of whom had seen service in the First World War. It was also seen as an excellent precursor to basic training for the under 18s in the regulars.

The idea was that with local knowledge these troops could engage the enemy invasion troops and hold them long enough for the regular forces to arrive.

A section of them, known as the Home Guard Auxiliary, were to – should the Germans have landed – go into hiding in their local areas and become saboteurs, and harassing commando-like troops. They were trained in all sorts of 'ungentlemanly warfare', as it was known, and had a life expectancy of only a couple of weeks maximum. They were to go to ground in secret 'hides' and sally forth from them to make life very difficult for the invaders.

The universal all ranks 'Cap GS' or Cap, General Service, or 'Cap, Ridiculous' as it became known, was worn from 1943 until well after the war had ended (shown left).

In August 1944, there came an order to make the Walking Out uniform smarter for the British soldier. As of this date, they could open the neck of the Battledress and sport a collar and tie, something that was previously only an officer affectation. Also, regimentally coloured Field Service Caps could be worn. Below we see a wedding from 1945, with pressed Battledress and open collars. It was an attempt to try and smarten up

Mobile field hospital in Carthage

what was essentially a fighting uniform. The Americans had a separate
Walking Out Dress.

In the image at the top of the page we see British officers, warrant
officers and sergeants wearing a mixture of lightweight 'East Of
Gibraltar' Khaki Drill, with the newer 'Jungle Greens'.

In the Far East campaigns of the Second World War it was found that
not only the web equipment rotted, but also the uniforms. It was also
noted that the Khaki Drill colour was not the best camouflage for jungle

warfare and thus, 'Junglies' were born. Some were of a lightweight green cotton, others were of a cloth called Aertex, which was a cooling fabric with a loose weave. In the picture underneath, we see what at first appears to be an army mobile field hospital but it is an RAF one (beware of assumptions in any part of family history research). They are all in Khaki Drill uniforms including the female nursing sisters. This, like one of the earlier RAF pictures, was taken in Carthage, North Africa, which is, of course, east of Gibraltar.

The introduction of the 1949 pattern battledress, seen below in 1954, was another attempt to smarten up a fighting uniform. Designed to be worn open, with collar and tie. It featured a shorter collar with a button hole on the open left collar flap. The centre buttons are covered, as per the 1937 Battledress, Serge, but the pocket ones are visible. It was still hot and uncomfortable to wear, but stayed warm when wet (and stank horribly) which is what serge had been doing for British soldiers since 1902. It wasn't until the 1960s that the 'layer principle' of clothing began to creep in.

The withdrawal of Scarlets in 1914 (except for regular bands and the Guards) and the continued use of Battledress without a specific parade dress was rectified with the (re)introduction of Number 1 dress. All forms

of dress were numbered, and as the best parade one it became No. 1. It was basically the patrol dress of years gone by which had now become universal. No. 2 dress was the new open collared service dress for other ranks. This picture is a coronation contingent from 1953 in No. 1s.

Below we see the shape of things to come; 'Woolly Pullies' with lightweight cotton trousers.

1st Battalion Northamptonshire Regiment Corps of Drums, Korea, 1955.

Jumpers and cardigans had been issued for many years but the so called 'Commando' jumper began to be issued in the Second World War. Here we see the Corps of Drums of the Northamptonshire Regiment in Korea in 1955. On their right arms they have a brassard with the regimental shoulder title and the badge of the Commonwealth Contingent in Korea.

Although they are part of a United Nations deployment, they are not wearing the blue berets and UN badge seen later on.

The above is yet another picture of the late pattern Service Dress. Again, the size of the peak is quite evident. Note that they are not wearing the long puttees associated with this form of dress. The bandmaster is in officer's Service Dress, and behind him is an officer in 'Battledress'. Sadly the pattern is indiscernible.

This is the band of the 5th Battalion of the Northamptonshire Regiment in Peterborough being inspected by the Colonel-in-Chief of the Regiment, HRH Princess Alice, the Duchess of Gloucester in 1955.

Equipment Carriers and Webbing

This section will focus on the main equipment carriers seen in family photos. There are, of course, a number of Victorian era white or buff leather sets that can be seen, as well as a number of trials and variations on the bandolier (the cross belt across the chest for ammunition).

Pictured on the right is the 1903 Pattern Leather equipment which was introduced after the Second Boer War because the pouches on issue during the war did not carry enough ammunition, and what was carried often fell out. This shows the basic set, with the infantry pattern bandolier. There was a mounted version of it which continued in use through, and indeed into, the Second World War, and had four further pouches on the rear. The belt can also be seen on uniforms (including the Home Guard and even the Women's Land Army) of the Second World War. On this belt are further ammunition pouches. This set was replaced by the 1908 webbing.

Seen below is the 1908 Pattern Web Equipment. This was quite revolutionary at the time, and far in advance of any other equipment carriers of the period. Firstly, it was made of a close weave heavy cotton material, with brass fitments to prevent fraying. Once covered in what was to be known as 'Blanco',

it became waterproof, and would not rot the same as leather variations.

The webbing, once correctly adjusted, was comfortable and easy to wear. It could be worn in a number of variations: marching order, drill order, and fighting order. The large and small packs were interchangeable and carried enough kit for the soldier to

fight until resupplied. It also didn't have to be taken apart to be taken off, and could be removed like a jacket. It could be partially adjusted on the march and the belt could even be undone for comfort. The belt itself was wide and helped with load distribution.

On the same picture (bottom of page 29), you may note that the rifle slings are also made of the same material. This webbing lasted until 1937 in front line use, and was only replaced for the necessity of more modern weapons. The picture is a platoon of soldiers marching 'easy', as the collars are undone. Note the equipment on the officer, which had to be purchased by the officer himself alongside his uniform.

In 1914, the regular army of Great Britain stood at 235,000 men. Of these, almost half were stationed overseas around the Empire. The ones at home were mustered and formed the British Expeditionary Force (BEF). The Territorial Force was formed of 14 infantry divisions and 14 mounted brigades. This force was intended for home defence as mentioned elsewhere, unless an individual had signed the Imperial Service Pledge. On 5 August the new Secretary of State for War, Earl Kitchener, asked for an additional 500,000 volunteers for the army. He foresaw that the war would not be 'over by Christmas' and that at least 70 infantry divisions would be needed for what he predicted would be at least a three year conflict.

After 'Kitchener's Call' there was a huge influx of men at the recruiting offices, with 1,186,357 men signing up between August and December 1914. In fact, Kitchener's initial numbers were far exceeded within 8 weeks. Problems with clothing have been discussed earlier, and the 1914 Leather Equipment was the answer to the initial lack of 1908 Webbing. It echoed the 19th century Slade Wallace, and elements of the 1903 and 1908 equipment, but was seen as a short term economy measure. In the early years, the belt is a signifier of a Kitchener volunteer. By 1918 a number of soldiers who were not necessarily from the influx of 1914-1915 used them as Walking Out belts. The chap shown opposite is, therefore, a Kitchener volunteer of the Cheshire Regiment.

In the mid 1930s, a series of trials were concluded which resulted in the adoption of a 'section light automatic' weapon, the 'Bren gun'. This resulted in the reorganisation of the rifle companies of the infantry battalions, in that the 4 platoons of 4 sections each were turned into 3 platoons of 3 sections. Each man in each section of 7 men would carry 1 to 2 Bren gun magazines in each pouch. This resulted in the adoption of a new pouch (below left) to replace the single pouches of the 1908 webbing. The belt was made narrower, but the large pack and haversack side were retained with new narrow fixings. The picture shows the 'basic' set. The soldier may be in Malta, near Mtarfa, or in North Africa. This webbing continued through the Korean War and up to 1958 when another new set was introduced. It also had to be 'blanco'd' to make it waterproof. In addition, there was a 1944 set, which was used mainly in jungle locations. Also, note the 1937 Khaki Field Service Cap, which is not dissimilar to the 1895 one previously shown.

Seen here, below right, in full marching order with sleeping bag atop the large pack, SR6 respirator in the side nylon bag, and the NBC equipment slung beneath the kidney pouches in the so called 'bum roll', is the 1958 Pattern Web Equipment, which was in use up until the early

37 web equipment

1990s. The helmet is the 1950s production MkIV with lowered rivets. This design was introduced in 1944, and lasted into the mid 1980s and the introduction of the first Kevlar helmet, the MkVI.

This equipment did not require Blanco, so it was not waterproofed. Instead, plastic bags and bin bags were used to line the pouches and large pack!

Also note that the subject is still wearing puttees, as per dress regulations in 1985. The short versions seen since the First World War in some theatres, and further expanded use in the Second World War.

This type of uniform and equipment can be seen in pictures of the Falklands War in 1982.

The cap badge is that of the Royal Anglian Regiment, and the subject was a member of the 2nd Battalion when this picture was taken. Note the black 'tombstone' behind the cap badge, which is a regimental peculiarity.

Some Badges in Date Order
Up until 1855 and the introduction of this new Shako hat (as seen in the below right picture), the design and height of the previous versions could be traced back to Waterloo and the headdress worn during the Peninsular

War by the British Army. This new version is much lower, and similar to the French kepi of the period. Its like can be seen on both sides of the contemporaneous American Civil War.

The star badge (opposite) is similar but smaller to the previous versions, and contains the number of the particular regiment. In this case we see Ensign (later Lieutenant Colonel) D.A. Anderson of the 58th Foot.

The image on the right is the last form of Shako plate, in use from 1869 to 1879. The pattern of the badge has changed, but retains the regimental number. Again, it was a kepi-like shako, slightly smaller than the last pattern. As the 'French look' fell out of favour, Great Britain would turn towards Germany and a spiked helmet, which is sometimes mistaken for a police helmet; although they share a common ancestor, they are quite different. This is the pattern of badge that the 24th Foot, the 2nd Warwickshires wore at Isandlwhana and Rorke's Drift in January 1879, and in the film, *Zulu*.

The 1878 Home Service Helmet and Plates

By the 1870s, the French style Shako had fallen out of fashion and Great Britain looked to Germany for inspiration. The spiked helmets of the Prussian army were much admired and the decision was taken to introduce a Home Service helmet, which was to last in various forms and is still in use today. Some regimental bands of the Corps of Army Music actually still wear a plastic variation. The helmet was of compressed cork and lined. It was decorated with brass roses at the side for the brass linked chinstrap, and a brass cruciform was on top, which supported the spike. Other Ranks' helmets were rounded at the front and officers had gilt badges with a pointed gilt peak and line from the rear top to bottom. The badge for Other Ranks

was exactly the same for all units excepting that the centre had regimental distinctions. Three are pictured above for comparison. All line infantry regiments wore these, with, of course, a couple of exceptions. The crown on this example is the Queen Victoria Crown (see the Crowns section at the beginning of this chapter). These crowns changed with the monarch, and some small changes were made to the regimental distinctions.

Interlude: The Glengarry and Field Service Cap

In 1874, following on from the fashion for all things 'Scottish' all line infantry regiments adopted the Glengarry with two ribbons down the back. This was to be used as an 'undress' item and not full dress, as the shakos and helmets were.

The problem for family historians looking at these photos is that the badges are almost all the same. A circlet surmounted by a crown or other regimental device such as the Keep of Gibraltar. Only the number in the centre was different.

Shown below are three examples.

The Glengarry was replaced by the blue Field Service Cap in the mid 1890s.

Above is the 1874 Glengarry, but it has a post 1881 helmet plate centre worn as a badge with a separate crown atop. It is not one of the pre 1881 Glengarry badges that can be seen on the previous page. The picture is indeed of the 1874 Glengarry, but it is from 1895, so technically it shouldn't be seen at this date. Note the visible ribbons hanging from the back.

The picture whence the close ups come is most informative and has a number of different uniform items in a single picture.

Here is an interesting anomaly, and the reason why I used variations on this particular badge at the beginning of this chapter. This is to show the differing crowns of the monarchs.

The chap on the right comes from the 1895 picture at the beginning of this chapter. He is wearing the Field Service Cap with Khaki Drill

uniform for those postings 'east of Gibraltar'. On his FSC though, is a collar badge, not a cap badge as one would expect.

There was a 'normal' sized cap badge available at this time, but for some reason, it is not being used in this picture. This is one of the anomalies one has to be aware of. Local orders, commanding officers' discretion and changes not reaching the far flung outposts for many, many months all have a bearing on dress. This is, of course, notwithstanding dress regulations as published!

Post Victorian 1878 Helmet Plates

Norfolk Regiment, 1902-1914

Helmet plate centre, Northamptonshire Regiment, 1902-1914

Band of the 2nd Battalion Royal Anglian Regiment, 1978-1994

Bandsman, 2nd Battalion Royal Anglian Regiment, 1984

On the previous page you may note the King's and Queen Elizabeth Crown helmet plates. The King's crown one was only really in use up until 1914 when Full Dress was withdrawn. The helmet plate centres reflect the subtle changes made to some of them in 1900/1902. The regimental bands retained them after the war, but more often than not they are seen in Service Dress or Battledress until the 1950s. After that, No. 1 dress is seen, although scarlets were not reintroduced until 1978 and helmets in 1979. They are in use today and can be seen on many of the former regimental bands who were disbanded in 1994, and some of today's CAMUS still wear them.

Years ago, a bandsman could spend his entire career with one band and be recruited and badged as thus. Today, CAMUS recruits and badges them, and they have no regimental affiliation, other than when posted to a particular band, such as one of the Household Division. The regimental styled bands are now few and far between and are reserve bands such as the Royal Anglian Band in Peterborough, which is the direct descendant of the 5th Battalion Northamptonshire band. They can be seen in a number of pictures throughout this book, along with pictures from the old 2nd Battalion Band of the Royal Anglian Regiment, which was marched off for the final time at Celle, Germany in March 1994.

Some Interesting Points to Note

This is an interesting picture on two accounts. Firstly, you may note that the badge of the Royal Sussex Regiment has been blackened. This is not an officer's badge (which is bronzed), this is a blackened other ranks badge, and, more than likely, all brass.

These badges were dulled by paint or boot black so as not to glint in the sun and draw the fire of snipers whilst in the trenches.

Secondly, you may note that the second button on the tunic is also blackened. This one has been covered by a black ribbon. It is known as a 'mourning button' and is worn to

Sussex with mourning button

commemorate a close relative (brother, father, etc) that had recently died during the conflict.

Note that this is only one button. If all the buttons down the front and on the pockets were black, this would identify him as a member of a rifles or light infantry regiment, which can be seen left.

Again, we see the so called 'economy' or, better yet, 'Tunic, Simplified' that was introduced from late 1914 and seen in 1915/1916.

To the left is a picture of a chap from the London Rifle Brigade, clearly showing the black buttons all over his tunic.

The black buttons are, as mentioned on the previous page, a sign that the wearer is a member of a Rifle regiment.

This is also interesting because he doesn't have brass shoulder titles, he has the earlier cloth ones.

He is also wearing a Tunic, Simplified, and may well be a Kitchener recruit.

It is not unusual for a soldier in the First World War to have served in more than one regiment or corps. The below images show my Great

Uncle Fred ('Little Uncle Fred') who served in both the Army Veterinary Corps (left) and the Durham Light Infantry (right) even though he was living in North London. Soldiers were sent where they were required, so not all went into their county regiments. Also beware of relatives with half a story or a completely incorrect one (*timeo familias et dona ferentes* – beware of the family bearing gifts, or even stories!). I was handed these photos by a cousin who insisted that it was our grandfather, and wrote as much on the back. Our grandfather (my maternal) was far too young to have been in the First World War, and a little bit of detective work solved the correct identity of this soldier. A lesson in that family stories are sometimes but 'Chinese whispers' and to never take at face value what is written on the back of photos, or what you are told by someone who was not around at the time who only has second or third hand guesses to hand down. As with all family history 'facts', make sure to confirm the fact three times from three different sources before it is entered into the tree.

Below are two pairs of legs which, at first glance, are exactly the same: long wrapped puttees. A closer inspection will actually show the difference between infantry and mounted troops.

On the left are the infantry ones, wound up the leg, from bottom to top.

On the right are the mounted, or someone who works with horses. These are wound down the leg, from top to bottom. The idea is that they do not rub against and unwind themselves on the horses flanks. You can also see the spurs and leather butterfly attachments on the boots.

Many people will argue that he's cavalry or artillery because of the mounted style puttees. This is erroneous. All regiments and corps of the army in the First World War used horses. All one can say is the subject of the photo worked with horses, unless there is any other identification present, as has been pointed out before.

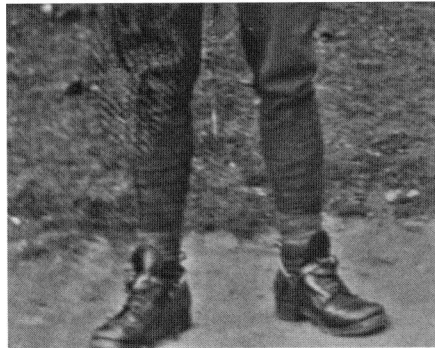

The below image shows how even a small postcard sized photo can show great detail. In the full-sized image we have a soldier posed with a photographer's prop in a snowy walled garden.

On closer inspection, we can see collar badges (never say never, but use the yardstick that virtually all infantry regiments didn't wear them in the First World War), and shoulder titles. The best bit, however, is the clarity of the badge. Under a magnifying glass – or better yet, a scanner – the badge is shown in great detail.

The hat itself is interesting. It is a variation on the 1907 Other Ranks Service Dress cap and is called a 'Gor Blimey'; supposedly thus named as when a sergeant major saw the first of these caps, he recoiled in horror at the unsoldierly like state of it. It features flaps tied or fixed across the top which can be lowered around the ears in inclement weather. They first appeared in 1915, in time for that winter. There is also an officer's version which, whilst retaining the general idea, is softer and fixed just over the peak with a belt-like affair.

The cap badge is quite patently that of the 7th (City of London) Royal Fusiliers, and this is confirmed by the fusilier grenades on the collar and

the same above the letters RF on the epaulette. They don't come much clearer and better than this for identification.

A couple of badges that I am frequently asked about are these munitions workers badges.

Shown on page 41 are the male and female versions from the First World War, both on their own and on clothing. The munitionette (lower picture) is in Khaki Drill overalls, but sometimes these young girls were seen in blue, and, in this case, these workers were known as 'Blue Belles'.

For completeness sake (there are Royal Naval Division badges of the First World War...) I have included a couple of pictures of Royal Navy seamen and petty officers. The above picture is from the

Second World War, and the 'Summer Rig' (white undershirts rather than black woollen ones in winter) is easily seen.

The badge of the petty officers (below, opposite), which are equal in rank to the army sergeant rank, is that of a 'fouled anchor' (it has rope wrapped around it) surmounted by a crown. They are also wearing jackets and ties.

RND seaman

Another fine and clear picture of a First World War sailor. This is another member of the Royal Naval Division (the others are in the main badge section), as can be seen by his 'cap tally' (the name band around his hat).

In wartime, the letters 'HMS' usually replaced the name of the ship the sailor was serving on, so any spies couldn't see which ships and therefore which flotillas were in port.

Not all ships named on the cap tally's were at sea, a number were shore based ships and were training establishments such as HMS *Dolphin*, the former submarine base at Fort Blockhouse on the Solent.

Chapter 2

BIRDS AND WINGS

Here are all the pictures that look like birds and wings. They can be derived from Prussian, German and Austrian imperial eagles, French imperial eagles captured in battle, the arms of a former colonel, and even for one badge, the American eagle!

They can be single headed, double headed, have things in their claws, be surrounded by a wreath or just a circle with a motto on.

The Royal Naval Division of the First World War has two contributions in this chapter: Hood and Hawke.

This division was made up of sailors and naval officers fighting as infantry in the trenches. They were not Royal Marines, but reservists from the Royal Navy. They wore khaki, but with the distinctions of the Royal Navy, hence the officers wore naval cuff ranks, and the petty officers wore the circle badge with the fouled anchor, topped by a crown in their caps.

The Royal Air Force badges can sometimes be confused with the First World War era Royal Naval Air Service, which amalgamated with the Royal Flying Corps to form the Royal Air Force on 1 April 1918, a date synonymous with jokes and japes from the other arms of the armed forces.

The 1st Kings Dragoon Guards were forced to change their cap badge in 1915. Their badge up until that date was from the arms of the Emperor Franz Joseph I of Austria. Not a good thing to wear in the middle of a war with that country. It was changed to the star shaped badge that can be found in the chapter 'Stars'.

The American eagle that is found in this chapter is obviously a rather strange one to find in a book about British cap badges. It is the badge of the 1st American Squadron of the British Home Guard during the Second World War. The badge is the same as that worn by US Army officers, but lacks the stars over the eagle's head. It was formed in 1940 and required a special order signed by the King himself to allow it to be part of the British Armed Forces, which it was until the stand down of the Home Guard in December 1944.

The Royal Bucks Hussars (Yeomanry) badge shows a swan, having a Duke's coronet round his neck, to which is attached a heavy gold chain. The Buckingham swan was the badge of the ancient families of De Bohn and Giffard who were Earls of Buckingham. It was also the badge of the Staffords who were the first Dukes of Buckingham.

The winged badges of the Special Air Service and the Parachute Regiment have been added for completeness.

Royal Air Force (Women's Auxiliary Air Force)

Royal Air Force Officers   *Royal Air Force W/O*   *Royal Air Force Officers*

Royal Scots Greys

Royal Bucks Hussars

Liverpool Pals, First World War

Mobile Defence Corps

Queen's Own Mercian
Yeomanry

Glider Pilot Regiment to 1953

Glider Pilot Regiment, post 1953

Army Air Corps, 1942-50

Army Air Corps post 1957

1st Royal Dragoons

1st King's Dragoon Guards

4th VB Gordon Highlanders

Bedfordshire Yeomanry

14th Kings Hussars

26th Hussars, 1941

Hawke Battalion Royal Naval Division

1st American Squadron Home Guard

14th Kings Hussars

Lanarkshire Yeomanry

1st King's Dragoon Guards Until 1915

Leeds Pals, First World War and Leeds Grammar School OTC

Hood Battalion, Royal Naval Division

4th VB Black Watch

The Special Air Service

The Parachute Regiment

Ayrshire Yeomanry

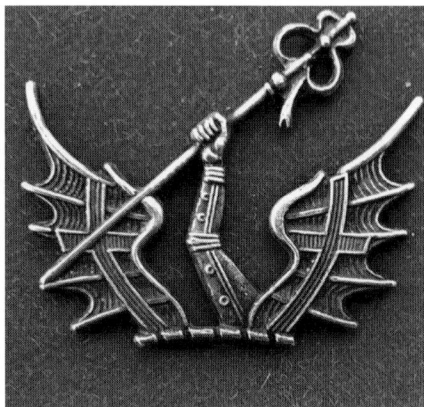

Honourable Artillery Company, post 1953

Chapter 3

BUGLE HORNS

The bugle horn is the sign of a light infantry unit. In the late 18th century, after learning the art of skirmishing from Prussian troops, the British Army formed light companies in all of the battalions of its line infantry.

As these troops acted independently and were 'fleet of foot', they needed something other than a drum to make signal. Thus the Prussian bugle horn was adopted. These light companies and regiments were championed by General Sir John Moore, who lost his life before Corruna in the Peninsular War.

They can be found on the badges of light regiments and the Rifle Volunteer Corps. Light troops are called riflemen instead of private.

A bugle horn is not, as supposed by some people, a 'powder horn'!

1st (King George's Own) Gurkha Rifles

2nd Bn Cameronians (Scottish Rifles)

3rd West Yorkshire Militia

Isle of Man Rifle Volunteers

10th (Princess Mary's Own) Gurkha Rifles

20th Sussex Militia

Above left and right: *Connaught Rangers Militia*

Above left and right: *Durham Light Infantry*

Duke of Cornwall's Light Infantry

1st VB Durham Light Infantry

Herefordshire Light Infantry

Highland Light Infantry

Highland Light Infantry, 2nd
Volunteer Battalion

King's Own Yorkshire Light Infantry

King's Shropshire Light Infantry

Liverpool Irish

Nottingham and Sherwood Rangers
Yeomanry

The Oxfordshire and Buckinghamshire
Light Infantry

Royal Marine Light Infantry

Royal Guernsey Light Infantry

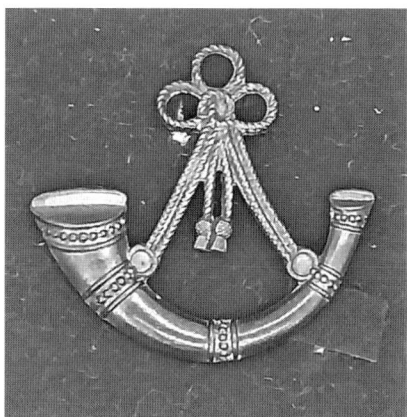
Sherwood Rangers Yeomanry

Somerset Light Infantry

Stafford Volunteer Rifles

Chapter 4

CASTLES

Castles on a badge can mean a number of things, from a local coat of arms to a local castle, or, in the case of four Gibraltar regiments, the keep and the key of the Gibraltar fortress. This is in recognition of the part they played in the defence of Gibraltar during the Great Siege of 24 June 1779 to 7 February 1783, the longest siege in military history.

The castle on the Cambridgeshire Regiment badge signifies the castle in the county town and also a defensive point on the river Cam.

Enniskillen Castle is depicted on the badges of the Inniskilling Regiments. Both the Fusiliers and the Dragoon Guards feature it as part of their badges.

Many units of the Norfolk Regiment have, at one time or another had a depiction of Norwich Castle upon their badges. One badge pictured in this book would look at first glance to be that of the Scots Guards. It is only on closer inspection that the centre and the words become visible. An interesting anomaly.

3rd Battalion Norfolk Rifle Volunteers   *6th (Inniskilling) Dragoons*

8th Battalion Hampshire
Regiment (Isle of Wight Rifles)

Pipers of the Royal Inniskilling Fusiliers

58th Foot Glengarry Badge,
1874-1881

Bedfordshire Yeomanry

Above left and right: *Cambridgeshire Regiment*

Devon and Dorset Regiment

Devonshire Regiment

Devonshire Regiment, pre 1902

Dorset Regiment

Officer Cadet of the Dorset Regiment

Dorset Regiment, pre 1900

Essex Regiment

4th Battalion Essex Regiment
(note the blank Egypt scroll)

Royal Inniskilling Fusiliers

King's Own Scottish Borderers

Loyal Suffolk Hussars Yeomanry

Northumberland Hussars
Yeomanry

Northampton Citizen Corps, First World War

Comparison for pre-1900 Regimental Keep (top) and post-1900 Standard Keep

Northamptonshire Regiment Glengarry Badges using helmet plate centre, 1895

Sgt Volunteer Battalion, Post 1902, Pre 1908

Sergeant major, 1880s, Northamptonshire Regiment

Comparative Sizes of Royal Anglian (top) and East Anglian Officers Badges

Royal Anglian Regiment

Suffolk soldier

East Anglian Brigade 1958-60, East Anglian Regiment 1960-64

The Suffolk Regiment

Above left: *Northamptonshire Regiment Helmet Plate 1881 to 1901*

Above middle and right: *Two variations of 4th (Territorial) Battalion The Northamptonshire Regiment*

A Kitchener volunteer of the Northamptonshire Regiment

Helmet Plate of the Royal Anglian Regiment Band from 1979 to 1994

The Home Service helmet was reintroduced almost exactly 100 years after it was first issued.

An AGAI of 1978 said that the regimental bands should return to their 'traditional' uniforms, i.e. scarlet tunics and (for the infantry bands) the spiked Home Service helmet.

Some bands reintroduced them almost immediately, and some, like the Cheshires, took several years to wear them again.

Most bands utilised the Other Ranks pattern, but the 2nd Royal Anglians issued the band with an officer's pattern helmet, complete with gilt peak to the front!

The felt backing to the badge is scarlet.

An oddity from the First World War and the Northamptonshire Regiment, called variously a VTC badge and a Territorial badge. It has been labelled in one book Daventry Volunteer Training Corps, or it could have been used once the Territorial Associations took over the VTC in the county. Note the T badges on the collar which would indicate Territorial Force (it was not renamed to the Territorial Army until 1921).

Chapter 5

CIRCLES AND OVALS

Above left and right: *15th King's Hussars*

Opposite above left and right: *Quite often young boys are seen, and this produces an outpouring of emotion. In the vast majority of cases, these boys are not 'soldiers', but belong to either a School Cadet or OTC unit, or as in this case a youth organisation. This lad (overleaf), like many others, is a member of the Church Lads Brigade, not a boy at the front! You will also see Scoutmasters and Boys Brigade leaders in military uniforms during the First World War.*

Above left and right: *The Middlesex Regiment*

*Princess Christian's Army Nursing
Reserve, Second Boer War*

First Aid Nursing Yeomanry

British Red Cross Society

Women's Legion

Women's Land Army, First World War

The Norfolk Regiment

Norfolk Regiment

14th King's Hussars

West Somerset Yeomanry

Queen's Regiment

Princess of Wales' Royal Regiment

King's Colonials South African

King's Colonials Australasian

Lancashire Hussars Yeomanry

Derbyshire Volunteer Home
Guard, First World War, VTC

Queen's Lancashire Regiment

York and Lancaster Regiment

4th Volunteer Battalion Hampshire Regiment

7th Battalion Hampshire Regiment

The Hampshire Regiment, 1900-1946

3rd Volunteer Battalion Hampshire Regiment

6th Battalion Hampshire Regiment

Lothian and Borders Horse Yeomanry Pipers

4th Battalion Seaforth Highlanders

Liverpool Scottish 1908-1937

Liverpool Scottish Post 1937

Yorkshire Hussars Yeomanry

Argyll and Sutherland Highlanders

Scots Guards Pipers

6th Volunteer Battalion Black Watch

Lovat's Scouts

Lowland Brigade, 1958-60

Highland Regiment, Second World War

Dorsetshire Regiment, post 1900

Dorsetshire Regiment, pre 1900

Northamptonshire Castle
variations

Northamptonshire Regiment

The Essex Regiment

Northamptonshire Volunteer Training Corps

Bedfordshire helmet plate

East Surrey helmet plate

Welbeck College, the army sixth form

Corps of Military Accountants

Army Legal Corps

14th King's Hussars

Warwickshire And Worcestershire Yeomanry

4th Volunteer Battalion Gordon
Highlanders

South Lancashire Regiment

Gloucestershire Regiment. Badge worn
on rear of hat.

South Wales Borderers

Queen Victoria School

National Motor Volunteers

Long Range Desert Group

Control Commission Germany

Women's Home Guard Auxiliary

Above left and right: Border Regiment Officers Variants

Women's Army Auxiliary Corps, First World War

Small Arms School Corps

2nd Northamptonshire Yeomanry, Second World War Only

64th Foot, 2nd Staffords (North Staffordshire)

5th Royal Irish Lancers

Royal Defence Corps

Forester Brigade, 1958

15th Kings Hussars

Above left and right: *2nd Battalion The Royal Anglian Regiment attached to the United Nations.*

The Battalion was part of UNFICYP, the United Nations Force In Cyprus. Note the regimental insignia on the shoulders still being worn, with the UN badge and British Contingent Union Flag badge.

The shirt was a local 'Private Purchase' not official uniform.

The beret is the UN Blue Beret specifically for operational identification.

Officer's pattern embroidered badge.

Chapter 6

CIRCLES AND OVALS SURMOUNTED WITH CROWNS

An officer of the Royal Army Medical Corps

Royal Army Medical Corps

Royal Army Ordnance Corps 1919 to 1947

Royal Army Ordnance Corps 1949 to 1955 (to 1992 with Queen's Crown)

Westmorland and Cumberland Yeomanry

Military Provost Staff Corps WW1

Army Apprentice School

8th Scottish Volunteer Battalion The Kings Liverpool Regiment 1902-1908

Drake Battalion, Royal Naval Division WW1

Welsh Guards, Sergeants and Band

1st Life Guards

2nd Life Guards

The Life Guards

Royal Horse Guards

4th Hussars Victorian

The Blues and Royals

5th Dragoon Guards

The Life Guards (1st and 2nd)

Royal Military College Sandhurst

Royal Electrical and Mechanical Engineers, 1st Pattern

8th Battalion West Yorkshire Regiment (Leeds Rifles)

18th Middlesex Rifle Volunteers (London Irish). Pre 1901, Victorian

19th Battalion Rifle Brigade

7th and 8th Battalion West
Yorkshire Regiment (Leeds Rifles)

19th County of London Regiment
(St Pancras)

17th County of London Regiment
(Poplar and Stepney Rifles). Pre 1926.

Rifle Brigade, 1903-10

Rifle Brigade, 1910-1936

Rifle Brigade, 1937-56

Rifle Brigade, 1956-58

7th (Robin Hoods) Battalion
Sherwood Foresters

7th Battalion West Yorkshire Leeds
Rifles

Royal Greenjackets

8th City of London Battalion Post Office
Rifles

Inns of Court OTC; Inns of Court Regiment; Inns of Court and County Yeomanry

Radnor Home Guard, 1952

Royal Army Chaplains Department, 2nd Pattern, Christian

Royal Army Chaplains Department, Jewish

Royal Army Veterinary Corps, 1918-Date

Above left and right: *Army Veterinary Corps, 1903-1918*

*Army Veterinary Department,
1902-1906*

*Army Dental Corps, 1st Pattern
1921-1946*

4th Hussars, Queen's Crown

7th Hussars

18th Hussars

Essex Yeomanry

24th Lancers

Army Air Corps, 1942-50

Glider Pilot Regiment, 1941-53

Glider Pilot Regiment, 1953-57

Army Air Corps, 1957-Date

*Army Remount Service,
1st Pattern*

Army Remount Service, 2nd Pattern

Northampton Citizen Corps, First World War

East Kent Yeomanry

Fife and Forfar Imperial Yeomanry

Royal Corps of Signals,
1st Pattern

2nd Battalion Monmouthshire
Regiment

Berkshire Officers' Beret Badge

Hertfordshire Militia Victorian

Hertfordshire Yeomanry

Hertfordshire Regiment

York and Lancaster Regiment

King's Own Royal Border
Regiment

Women's Royal Army Corps,
1949-1992

Royal Hampshire Regiment,
1946-1992

East Lancashire Regiment

City of London Yeomanry
Rough Riders, 1st Pattern

City of London Yeomanry,
2nd Pattern

Royal Hospital Chelsea
(Chelsea Pensioners)

Dorset Yeomanry (Modern)

Northumberland Hussars

Royal Buckinghamshire Hussars
Yeomanry

Royal Military Academy
Sandhurst, Pre 1953

Royal Military Academy, 1953-date

Surrey Yeomanry

Yorkshire Dragoons Yeomanry

Guards Machine Gun Regiment

25th County of London Cyclists

Lancastrian Brigade

Essex Yeomanry

Army Catering Corps, 2nd Pattern

2nd Battalion Duke Of Wellingtons
Regiment, 1881-1902

23rd County of London
Yeomanry (Sharpshooters),
Armoured Car Company

3rd County of London Yeomanry
(Sharpshooters)

Royal Horse Artillery, George VI
monogram changed with Monarch
from Edward VII To Date.

Hampshire Carabiniers Yeomanry

6th Dragoon Guards

Queen Alexandra's Imperial Military Nursing Service, 1902-1949 (Female)

Queen Alexandra's Royal Army Nursing Corps, 1949-Date 1949-1952 with Kings Crown (Female only until 1992)

The London Rifle Brigade, 5th London Regiment

London Rifle Brigade 1902-1920

Territorial Force Nursing Service, 1908-1920 (left) and Territorial Army Nursing Service, 1920-1949 (right)

Women's Land Army, First World War

London Rifle Brigade 1920-1956

London Rifle Brigade Cadets

Navy and Army Canteen Board

Navy Army and Air Force Institutes

Above left and right: *Royal Navy Petty Officers*

Corps Of Royal Engineers: Variations by Monarch: Queen Victoria—Current Issue

Badges That Can Be Confused With Royal Engineers

British West Indies Regiment
(Caribbean Volunteers,
First World War)

10th County Of London Paddington
Rifles

Queen's Own Dorset Yeomanry

King's Own Malta Regiment

Above left and right: 18th Hussars (Two variants)

13th Hussars

1st Sussex Volunteer Rifle Corps

Duke of Lancaster's Yeomanry

Legion of Frontiersmen

Suffolk Regiment

8th Battalion Hampshire
Regiment, Isle of Wight Rifles

Kings Own Scottish Borderers

Scottish Horse 2nd Pattern, 1903

Hampshire Cyclist Battalion

Army Cyclist Corps

Northern Cyclist Battalion

Royal Flying Corps

Royal Air Force

Queen's Bays

Queen Mary's Army Auxiliary Corps,
First World War (Female)

Royal Armoured Corps, 1st Pattern

Leicestershire Imperial Yeomanry

Leicestershire Yeomanry

Auxiliary Territorial Service, 1938-1949 (female)

Isle of Man Home Guard, 1952

South London Volunteer Training Corps (This badge was used by many units, only the name on the scroll changed)

Royal Army Dental Corps, 2nd Pattern

Royal Observer Corps

Queen's Own Mercian Yeomanry

Queen's Own Worcestershire
Hussars Yeomanry

National Defence Company

Tank Corps, First World War

Royal Tank Corps, 1924
(withdrawn same year)

Royal Tank Corps, 1924-1939
and Royal Tank Regiment,
1939-Date

1st Armoured Motor Battery,
Mesopotamia, First World War

Grenadier Guards, Sergeants and Bands

Royal Armoured Corps, 2nd Pattern

Guards Division, Officer Training Battalion

Nottingham and Sherwood Rangers Yeomanry

Army Catering Corps, 1st Pattern

Shropshire Yeomanry

Yorkshire Dragoons Yeomary

Women's Land Army, Second World War

Royal Pioneer Corps, 2nd Pattern

Royal Military Police, First World War

Royal Military Police, Post 1952

Gurkha Military Police

Royal Military Academy,
Woolwich

Queen Alexandra's Imperial
Military Nursing Service
(Reserve), 1908-1949 (Female)

Air Raid Precautions (ARP),
Second World War

Northamptonshire Regiment
Collar Badge, used as Cap Badge

Queens Royal Irish Hussars

Kent Artillery Militia

Royal Irish Rifles Pipers, 1902-1922

Royal Irish Fusiliers

Victorian Glengarry Badges, a selection

48th Foot Northamptonshire

58th Foot Rutlandshire

Post 1881 Northamptonshire

Pre 1881 35th Foot Royal Sussex

Pre 1898 Army Medical Department

Connaught Rangers

2nd Volunteer Battalion West Yorkshire

4th Volunteer Battalion East Surrey Regiment

Above left: *5th Volunteer Battalion Black Watch*

Above right: *Cinque Ports Volunteer Rifles*

Right: *Bedfordshire Regiment Officers*

Chapter 7

COATS OF ARMS AND SHIELDS

Above left and right: *Labour Corps, VTC Generic First World War*

This badge causes much discussion and disagreement. What is quite clear is that there was no General Service Corps in the First World War. The GSC was not formed until 1942.

In the First World War as in the Second, there was a General List for unattached officers, but not the rank and file.

If the Royal Coat of Arms is on an officer's Service Dress uniform, he is on the General List. If it is on the uniform of a First World War soldier, he is one of a couple of things. He is either in the Labour Corps, or he could be a Volunteer Training Corps (First World War Home Guard) just before they converted to the County Line Infantry Regiment badges in 1918.

If the picture is from the Second World War, and it is on the head dress, it is General Service Corps. This was formed in 1942 to accept and train the conscription soldiers, as opposed to going to a Regimental Depot for Basic Training. Camps were set up around the country and recruits were sent and allocated a true 'Service Number'. At the end of this basic training they were then allocated to a regiment or Corps dependent upon their skills and requirements of the service.

If the badge is worn on the wrist or arm, the subject is a regimental sergeant major, or other warrant officer class 1, and with a wreath around it, a 'conductor'.

Lincolnshire Yeomanry

Leeds Pals, First World War Or Leeds Grammar School OTC

Upper Thames Patrol, Second World War, Home Guard

Royal Scots Fusiliers

Manchester Regiment, 1900-1922

Cardiff Commercials ('Pals' Battalion), First World War

Westminster Dragoons Yeomanry

Exeter Rifle Volunteers

Essex Yeomanry, 1st Pattern

Essex Yeomanry, 2nd Pattern

Shropshire Yeomanry

Northampton Citizen Corps,
Volunteer Training Corps

Cinque Ports, Volunteer Rifles

Sussex Yeomanry

Royal Jersey Light Infantry

City of London Yeomanry
Rough Riders, 1st Pattern

City of London Yeomanry Rough
Riders, 2nd Pattern

Army Ordnance Corps Pre 1919

Royal Army Ordnance Corps 1919 to 1947

Royal Army Ordnance Corps 1949 to 1955 (to 1992 with Queen's Crown)

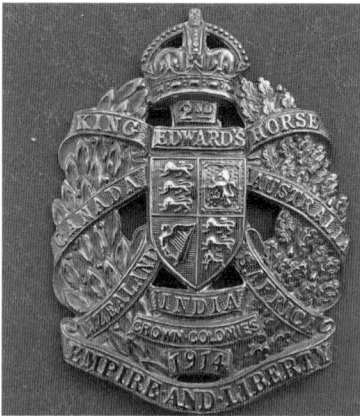

Above left and right: *King Edward's Horse (The Kings Overseas Dominions Regiment), Two Variants*

London Rifle Brigade Cadets

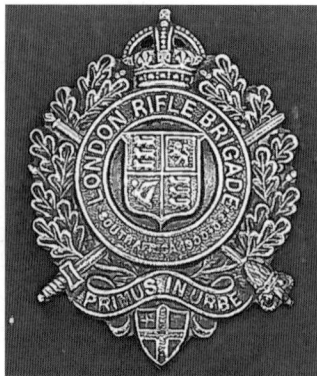

London Rifle Brigade, 1st Pattern

London Rifle Brigade, 2nd Pattern

1st King's Dragoon Guards

13th County of London Battalion, The Kensingtons

Above left: *Legion of Frontiersmen, a paramilitary style organisation that provided a Battalion to the Royal Fusiliers in the First World War*

Above right: *Women's Home Defence, Second World War. Most members joined the Home Guard once women were allowed*

Right: *British Red Cross Society*

Chapter 8

CROSS

Above left and right: *Army Chaplains' Department, First World War*

Buckinghamshire Battalion, Oxfordshire and Buckinghamshire Light Infantry

The King's Royal Rifle Corps

*9th (County Of London)
Battalion, Queen Victoria's Rifles*

*16th County of London Queen's
Westminster Rifles, post 1922*

*The Kings Royal Rifle Corps, pre
1901*

*21st (County of London)
Regiment, 1st Surrey Rifles*

Above left and right: *16th (County of London) Queen's Westminster
Rifles, 1902-1922 (Two Versions)*

The King's Royal Rifle Corps,
post 1902

Royal East Kent Mounted Rifles
Yeomanry

Church Lads' Brigade. Original
pattern affiliated to the Kings Royal
Rifle Corps (Schoolboys) Cadets

11th (County of London)
Regiment, Finsbury Rifles

Above left and right: *11th (County of London) Regiment, The Rangers*

West Kent Rifles, pre 1901

6th City of London Battalion

7th (Leeds Rifles) Battalion, West
Yorkshire Regiment

7th and 8th Battalion, West
Yorkshire Regiment (Leeds Rifles)

8th Battalion, West Yorkshire Regiment
(Leeds Rifles)

19th County of London Regiment
(St Pancras)

17th (County of London) Poplar and
Stepney Rifles, pre 1926

7th (Robin Hood's) Battalion,
Sherwood Foresters

8th City of London Battalion, Post
Office Rifles

Royal Army Chaplains'
Department, 2nd Pattern,
Christian

Royal Greenjackets

Radnor Home Guard, 1952

18th Middlesex Rifle Volunteers
(London Irish), pre 1901

Inns of Court OTC; Inns of
Court Regiment; Inns of Court
and County Yeomanry

The Rifle Brigade from 1903-10

The Rifle Brigade, 1910-36

The Rifle Brigade, 1937-56

The Rifle Brigade, 1956-58

The Rifle Brigade, 19th Bn

Lowland Brigade, 1958

The Black Watch, (The Royal Highlanders)

Highland Cyclist Battalion

Above left and right: *Scottish Horse (two variants)*

14th County of London Battalion, London Scottish

Lowland Regiment, Second World War

Highland Regiment, Second World War

Tyneside Scottish, 1916 pattern

Above left and right: *Cameron Highlanders (two variants)*

Above left and right: *Liverpool Scottish (two variants)*

92nd Gordon Highlanders, Victorian

Highland Brigade, 1958

Highland Light Infantry

2nd Volunteer Battalion, Highland Light Infantry

Scots Guards

Royal Scots

3rd Norfolk Rifle Volunteer Corps (Victorian)

Royal Scots Fusiliers Pipers

King's Own Scottish Borderers

Derbyshire Regiment

Above left and right: *Nottinghamshire and Derbyshire Regiment, crown variants*

Forester Brigade, 1958

5th (Cinque Ports) Battalion, Royal Sussex Regiment

Bedfordshire Regiment

Bedfordshire Regiment

Bedfordshire Regiment variant

Bedfordshire and Hertfordshire Regiment

Duke of Edinburgh's Regiment

The Wiltshire Regiment

The Royal Gloucestershire, Berkshire and Wiltshire Regiment, 1994-2007

Above left and right: *Territorial Battalions of the Border Regiment, 4th Cumberland and 5th Westmorland*

Above left and right: *The Border Regiment Officers' Variants*

The Border Regiment

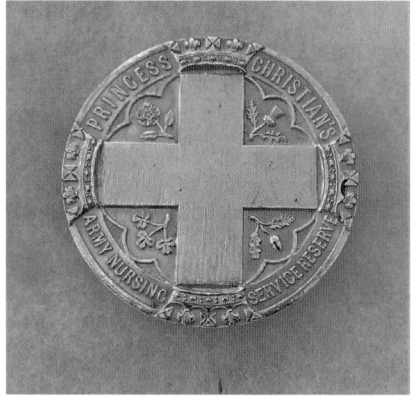

Princess Christian's Army Nursing Service Reserve 2nd Boer War

British Red Cross Society

Queen Alexandra's Imperial Military Nursing Service (QAIMNS), 1902-1949 (Female)

Above left and right: First Aid Nursing Yeomanry (two variants)

QAIMNS Tippet (cape) Badge (medal)

Queen Alexandra's Royal Army Nursing Corps, 1949-Date. From 1949-1952 with Kings Crown

Medical Staff Corps up to 1898 and the formation of the Royal Army Medical Corps

Welbeck College, the Army sixth form

Church Lads' Brigade, 2nd Pattern   *King's Own Malta Regiment*

Above left and right: *Alexandra, Princess Of Wales' Own (Yorkshire Regiment).*
Green Howards (variants)

Chapter 9

DRAGONS

Dragons are mostly found on Welsh badges. Exceptions include the Royal Berkshire Regiment and their descendant regiments. This badge was gained for service in China. There are a couple of others that used dragons, including the North Somerset Yeomanry, which is probably more of an Arthurian connection.

Above left and right: *Royal Berkshire Regiment*

Right: *Royal East Kent Regiment, The Buffs*

4th Battalion Royal East Kent Regiment, The Buffs

11th Battalion Border Regiment, 'Lonsdales'

1st Battalion Monmouthshire Regiment

3rd Battalion Monmouthshire Regiment

Above left and right: *2nd Battalion Monmouthshire Regiment (two variants)*

Monmouthshire Imperial Yeomanry

Queen's Regiment

Princess of Wales' Royal
Regiment

Brecknockshire Battalion, South Wales
Borderers

West Somerset Yeomanry

Royal Regiment of Fusiliers

Ayrshire Yeomanry

Royal Army Dental Corps,
1946-1953. 1953 – date with
Queen's Crown

Royal Berkshire Regiment

Royal Berkshire Officer's Beret Badge

Chapter 10

FEATHERS

One of the most difficult badges to identify: The Prince of Wales feathers, or Plume of Feathers, which is featured on no less than 36 of the 37 badges pictured in this chapter. It is often said when people are trying to identify a badge with feathers, that it is Welsh. Well yes, sometimes, but not always. Many of the badges are almost identical except for the wording on the scroll or the angle of the scrolls that contain the motto, 'Ich Dien' (I serve). Compare, for example, the 3rd Dragoon Guards, with the 12th Royal Lancers, the Cheshire Yeomanry (or the Boer War incarnation, the Earl of Chester's Imperial Yeomanry), the Denbigh Hussars, the Flint and Denbigh Hussars, the Royal Hussars, etc. Without further information, it's really difficult to put a name to a soldier with this form of badge, but a little digging around may give you some leads, which may lead you to the correct individual in your family. Some of the information may be quite easy, but one will have to date the uniform and compare with reserve forces, such as the yeomanry, and regular forces, along with the dates of the photos. Whilst this is something of a 'dark art', hopefully this book can give you a few pointers as to what to look for.

The badges that don't solely feature the feathers are a lot easier, especially when cross referenced with the other features on the badge. The Royal Welsh (Welch) Fusiliers badge also features a grenade (of the early sort) and flames, although when detail is lacking on a photo or someone has taken a photo of a photocopy, or it has been colourised, this fusilier badge may prove just as elusive!

The picture above exemplifies the problems inherent in some forms of badges, especially those within this chapter. The scroll at the bottom of the feathers helps to narrow down the search, but without knowing the name of the individual, or a better view of what is written on the scroll, or indeed a full picture; all we can say is that he is from one of about eleven units, and from the period 1907 to circa 1921.

Middlesex Regiment

Royal Sussex Regiment

Royal Welch (Welsh) Fusiliers

South Lancashire Regiment

64th Foot, 2nd Staffords (North Staffordshire)

Royal Monmouth Royal Engineers

Connaught Rangers Militia variant

1st King George's Own Gurkha Rifles

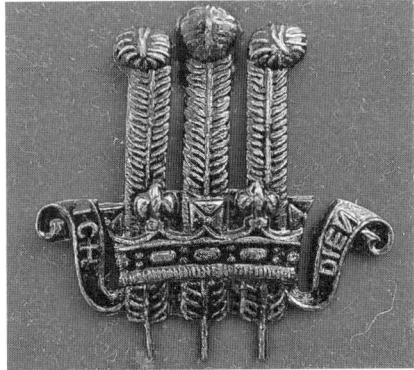

2nd King Edward's Own Gurkha Rifles

Donegal Militia

3rd Carabiniers

10th Imperial Yeomanry

Yorkshire Dragoons Yeomanry

12th Lancers

Imperial Hospital Yeomanry

The Leinster Regiment

15th County of London Civil Service Rifles

Royal Regiment of Wales

Welsh Brigade, 1958

Royal Wiltshire Yeomanry

10th Royal Hussars

3rd Dragoon Guards

12th Royal Lancers

The Royal Hussars

Glamorgan Imperial Yeomanry

Caernarvon and Denbigh Yeomanry

Glamorgan Yeomanry

Flint and Denbigh Yeomanry

Pembroke Yeomanry

Denbighshire Hussars Yeomanry

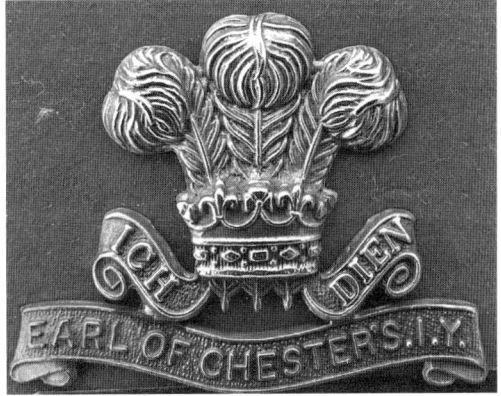

Earl of Chester's Imperial Yeomanry

Cheshire Yeomanry

The Welsh Regiment

Queen's Regiment

Princess of Wales' Royal Regiment

4th Prince Of Wales Gurkha Rifles

King's Colonials side of hat badge

Chapter 11

FIGURES AND FACES

This chapter includes badges that include a full figure, such as the Women's Legion, or just faces, as in the images of Mars and Minerva on the badge of the Artist's Rifles.

The Artist's Rifles are an intriguing unit having first appeared in 1859 as a Rifle Volunteer Corps. Founded, as were many hundreds of similar units across the country, due to a mid 19th century fear of another French invasion attempt. The Artist's Rifles contained some very famous artists, amongst them Frederic Lord Leighton, Dante Gabriel Rosetti, and most of the Pre Raphaelite Brotherhood. Today they are known as 21 Special Air Service Regiment (Artists).

The Norfolk Regiment, 1900-1937

The Norfolk Regiment, 1900-1937

The Norfolk Regiment helmet plate

The Royal Norfolk Regiment, 1937-1959

The Norfolk Regiment, officers variant

Above left and right: *Cameron Highlanders (two variants)*

Royal Scots Fusiliers Pipers

Liverpool Scottish, post 1937

The Royal Corps of Signals, 1920-1947

Above left and right: *28th (County of London) The Artist's Rifles*

The Royal Corps of Signals, 1947-Date (1953-Date with Queen's Crown)

Highland Cyclist Battalion

The Black Watch, The Royal Highlanders

Inns of Court Yeomanry

Royal Observer Corps

Women's Legion

Chapter 12

FLOWERS AND PLANTS

There are many forms of plants displayed on badges. Most of them have county or country affiliations such as the leek, the badge of the Welsh Guards and the Welsh Horse Yeomanry.

Several badges show either the red rose of Lancaster or the white of York. The Intelligence Corps uses the combined Tudor Rose. The Canadian General Service badge is that of the maple leaf.

A couple of the Irish regimental badges feature the shamrock.

The Lothian Yeomanry have a wheatsheaf, a sign of the border farmlands.

The acorn on the badge of the Cheshire Regiment dates back to George II, and the 1743 battle of Dettingen, where he was the last British monarch to command troops in the field. At one point the king was pursued by the French cavalry. A contingent of infantry gathered around him under an oak tree and drove the French away. The king plucked a leaf from the tree and handed it to the officer commanding, ordering that the regiment wear it in their head dress in memory of their 'gallant conduct'.

The South Notts Hussars also wear an acorn with an oak leaf, this relates to Sherwood Forest where they recruited.

Lancashire Hussars Imperial Yeomanry   *Lancashire Hussars Yeomanry*

Above left and right: *Yorkshire Dragoons Yeomanry (two variations)*

Lancastrian Brigade, 1958   *Yorkshire Hussars Yeomanry*

3rd Volunteer Battalion, Hampshire Regiment

Derbyshire Volunteer Home Guard VTC, First World War

6th Battalion Hampshire Regiment

Above left and right: *Loyal North Lancashire Regiment*

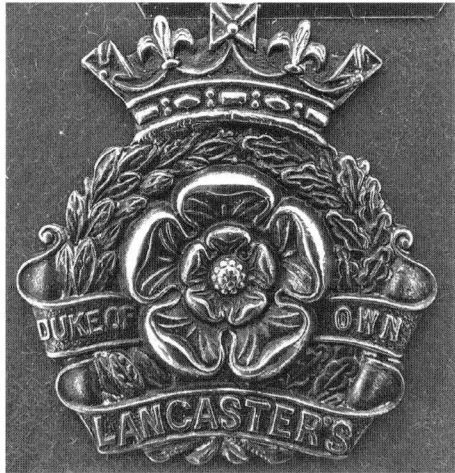

Intelligence Corps

Duke of Lancaster's Yeomanry

Queen's Lancashire Regiment

South Nottinghamshire Hussars Yeomanry

Above left and right and below: *Cheshire Regiment (two variants)*

Women's Land Army, First World War *Women's Land Army, Second World War*

Lothian and Borders Horse Yeomanry

Lothian and Borders Horse Yeomanry Pipers

Lothian and Berwick Imperial Yeomanry

Lothian and Borders Horse Yeomanry

Welsh Guards, Sergeants and Band

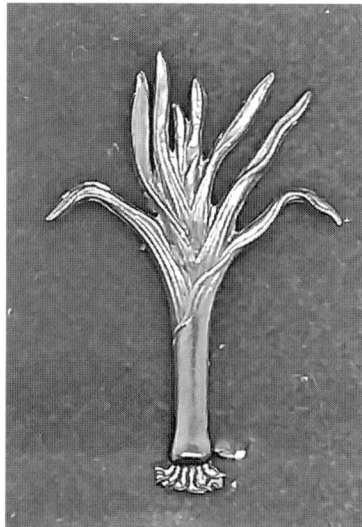

Welsh Guards

Welsh Horse Yeomanry

South Irish Horse Yeomanry

14th Battalion Royal Irish Rifles

9th Irish Horse Yeomanry

Lowland Regiment, Second World War

Lowland Brigade, 1958

5th Volunteer Battalion, The Black Watch

Worcestershire Hussars Yeomanry

Princess of Wales Royal Regiment

Canadian General Service Badge

New Zealand Expeditionary Force, 1914-1915

Westmorland and Cumberland Yeomanry

Chapter 13

GRENADES AND FLAMES

These represent the late 18th and early 19th century grenades once carried by the Grenadier companies of the British infantry. They were a cumbersome item and the fuse needed to be lit properly before being deployed. Most people are now familiar with the grenade developed during the First World War (Mills Bomb), and for many years the name 'Bomber' was applied to those who threw grenades.

The Fusilier Regiments' name comes directly from the original French word for a flintlock musket. These replaced the matchlock musket in around 1680 in the British army. The first regiment to bear the name was the 7th (City of London) Royal Fusiliers. The title was granted upon the raising of the regiment in 1685.

The infantry units of the Honourable Artillery Company, the senior regiment in the Army Reserve (Territorial Army) wear the grenade, and it can often be mistaken for either Grenadier Guards or a Fusilier regiment on pictures.

Northumberland Fusiliers

Northumberland Fusiliers

From 1900 to 1920, the title Royal Welsh Fusiliers was used, after this date the old spelling of 'Welch' was used.

The Royal Fusiliers

1st Volunteer Battalion, The Royal Fusiliers

Above left and right: *Grenadier Guards Variants*

Above left and right: *Honourable Artillery Company Variants*

The Royal Regiment of Fusiliers

25th Battalion The Royal Fusiliers, 'Legion of Frontiersmen', First World War

Lancashire Fusiliers

Royal Dublin Fusiliers

Royal Munster Fusiliers

Royal Inniskilling Fusiliers

Royal Irish Fusiliers

7th (City of London) Battalion, The London Regiment

Royal Scots Fusiliers

Above left, middle and right: *Royal Marine Artillery variants*

Royal Marine Artillery 1890s Pillbox Cap Ranks. Corporal Left, Sergeant Right

Kent Artillery Militia

Royal Artillery Field Service Cap Badge (same as the collar badge)

Corps of Gurkha Engineers

Royal Army Educational Corps, Pre 1952

Royal Army Educational Corps, Post 1952

Chapter 14

GUNS

Several units can be found with a form of gun on their badge. These range from the Royal Artillery, who count their guns as the Regimental Colours, the carbines (short cavalry rifles) of the Carabiniers, the crossed rifles of the Sharpshooters (3rd County of London), and the crossed Vickers machine guns of the Machine Gun Corps. The Heavy Section of the MGC became the Tank Corps. The Royal Naval Division Machine Guns had a badge which was essentially the same as the MGC but with the letters RND attached at the bottom. The Mounted Machine Gun Corps of the cavalry divisions also had a similar badge, with the letters MMG at the bottom of the crossed Vickers.

The Guards Division, always liking to be different, had their own badge for their own Machine Gun Regiment.

The School of Musketry had two crossed rifles surmounted by a crown, which was also the proficiency badge worn on the lower arm for the best shot in a battalion.

One small oddity which I have added, is the Women's Home Defence Force of the Second World War. This is a small lapel badge worn by the ladies recruited by the Labour MP for Fulham Dr Edith Summerskill, known to them as 'Flossie Bang Bang', who formed an unofficial, quasi paramilitary force in December 1941. Many of the members went on to become members of the Women's Home Guard Auxiliary when their membership of the Home Guard was permitted by the War Office in 1943.

Up until the 1920s the Royal Artillery was divided into the Royal Garrison, the Royal Field and the Royal Horse Artillery. All of these branches wore the same cap badge and all of them used horse. Therefore as in the picture overleaf, a chap with mounted wound puttees with spurs (and usually a 1903 Bandolier) cannot be pinned down to Royal Horse Artillery as many would say. The white lanyard prior to the mid 1920s cannot be said to be an Artillery 'thing' either. This all not withstanding, the chap pictured is known to be Royal Field Artillery. This was elucidated through due diligence of records, not via a guess.

Above left and right: *The Royal Regiment of Artillery.*

Royal Artillery Other Ranks service dress cap 1907-1921

Honourable Artillery Company

Royal Artillery Territorial Force, post 1908

1st Hampshire Royal Garrison Artillery Volunteers, pre 1908

Above and below: *3rd County of London Yeomanry 'Sharpshooters'*

6th Dragoon Guards

3rd Carabiniers

Hampshire Carabiniers

School of Musketry

Machine Gun Corps

Above left and right: Guards Machine Gun Regiment

Mounted Machine Gun Corps

Royal Naval Division Machine Gun Battalion

Royal Military Academy, Woolwich

Small Arms School Corps

Women's Home Defence

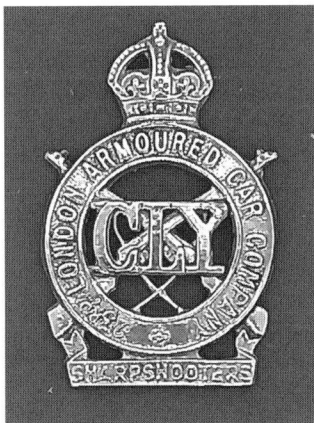

23rd County Of London
Yeomanry Sharpshooters
Armoured Car Company

South London Volunteer Training Corps
(This badge was used by many units,
only the name on the scroll changed)

Chapter 15

HARPS

If a badge features a harp, the regiment certainly has an Irish connection. This is not to say that the picture is of the Irish Army. Up until 1922 and the creation of the Irish Free State, the 32 counties and 4 provinces, Ulster, Munster, Leinster and Connaught were all part of Great Britain, and provided soldiers for the British Army. A wealth of fine regiments fought with honour and distinction throughout the ages. Now only Ulster remains within the United Kingdom and the only infantry regiment left is the Royal Irish Rifles. The British Army still takes recruits from the south but all of the other regiments have marched off the parade ground and into the mists of time. The Irish Guards are of course still extant but the last of the Irish cavalry regiments, The Queen's Royal Irish Hussars, was amalgamated in 1993.

Other badges come from the areas of high Irish descent populations in England, such as the Liverpool Irish, The London Irish and The Tyneside Irish. These were originally territorial units, and of course London also had The London Welsh and The London Scottish…Rugby fans may see a link here…

Above left and right: *8th King's Royal Irish Hussars*

*18th County of London
London Irish (to 1937)*

Ulster Defence Regiment

*Ulster Home Guard, 1940-1945
(Yes, it is the same badge!)*

Royal Irish Rifles, Victorian

*Royal Irish Rifles, Pipers
1902-1922*

*Royal Ulster Rifles, also Royal
Irish Rifles*

North Irish Brigade, 1958

Royal Irish Rangers

Tyneside Irish, First World War

Above left, right and below left, right: *Connaught Rangers*

Above left and right: *8th Irish Battalion Kings Liverpool Regiment (Liverpool Irish)*

North Irish Horse Yeomanry

Queen's Royal Irish Hussars

Royal Irish Fusiliers

Chapter 16

HORSES

Above left and right: *1st Northamptonshire Yeomanry*

2nd Northamptonshire Yeomanry, 1939-1945

The King's (Liverpool) Regiment variant

King's Regiment

The King's (Liverpool) Regiment variant

West Yorkshire Regiment, 1st Volunteer Battalion

Above left and right: *West Yorkshire Regiment*

Above left, middle and right: *Army Remount Service, three variants*

3rd The King's Own Hussars

East Kent Yeomanry

Fife and Forfar Imperial
Yeomanry

Royal West Kent Regiment

20th (County of London) Blackheath and
Woolwich

Kent Cyclist Battalion

West Kent Yeomanry

West Yorkshire Regiment,
2nd Volunteer Battalion

Liverpool Scottish, 1908-1937

5th Dragoon Guards

Royal Electrical and
Mechanical Engineers

6th Volunteer Battalion, Black Watch

Fife and Forfar Scottish Horse

Royal East Kent Mounted Rifles

Berkshire Imperial Yeomanry

Chapter 17

KNIVES, DAGGERS AND SWORDS

1st King George's Own Gurkha Rifles

3rd Queen Alexandra's Own Gurkha Rifles

4th Prince of Wales' Own Gurkha Rifles

5th Royal Gurkha Rifles

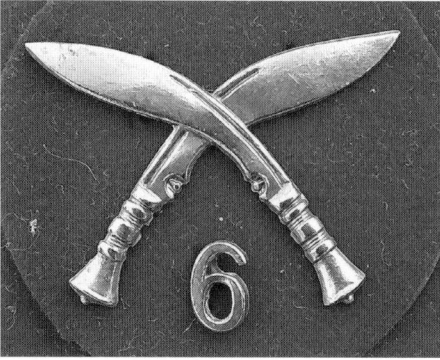

6th Gurkha Rifles

6th Queen Elizabeth's Own Gurkha Rifles

7th Gurkha Rifles

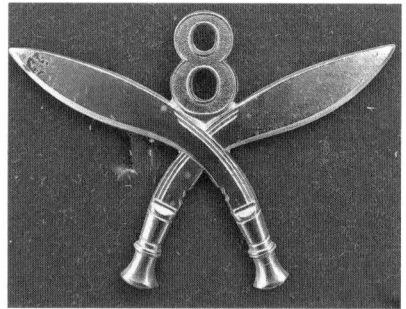

8th Gurkha Rifles

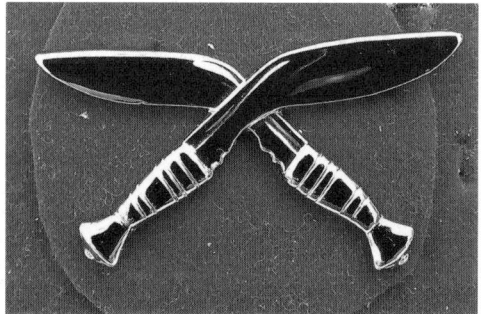

Above left: 9th Gurkha Rifles

Above right: Gurkha Staff Band

Left: Royal Gurkha Rifles

Above left and right: *Gurkha Signals*

Gurkha Military Police

25th Dragoons

Gurkha Transport Regiment

Corps of Gurkha Engineers

Infantry Training Battalions

Welbeck College Army Sixth Form

Above left: *Special Air Service*

Above right: *No. 2 Commando*

Left: *V Force*

Church Lads' Brigade

Royal Pioneer Corps, 2nd Pattern

Army Apprentice School

Army Physical Training Corps (Royal from 2010)

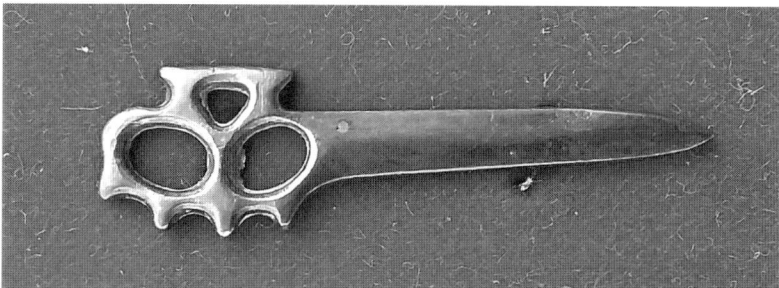

Nos 50-52 Commando

Chapter 18

LETTERS, MONOGRAMS AND ROMAN NUMERALS

Expeditionary Forces Canteen (The precursors of the NAAFI and EFI)

Forage Corps

Non Combatant Corps

All three badges are shoulder titles worn as cap badges

Royal Military School Of Music, Kneller Hall

King's Colonials (side of hat)

Above left and right: *Army Pay Corps (two variants)*

Above left, right and right:
Alexandra, Princess Of Wales' Own (Yorkshire Regiment), The Green Howards

Above left, right and below left, right: *Norfolk Yeomanry, Reigning Monarch variations*

Above left and right: *Royal Air Force*

Women's Home Guard Auxiliary

Royal Flying Corps

Queen's Bays

Royal Armoured Corps, 1st Pattern

Queen Mary's Army Auxiliary Corps,
First World War (female)

Auxiliary Territorial Service, 1938-1949
(female)

*Royal Military College
Sandhurst*

Army Dental Corps, 1921-1946

*Army Veterinary Department,
1902-1906*

*Army Veterinary Corps,
1903-1918*

1st Life Guards

2nd Life Guards

1st and 2nd Life Guards

Royal Horse Guards

The Life Guards

The Blues and Royals

18th Hussars

Grenadier Guards, Sergeants and Band

National Defence Company

Women's Army Auxiliary Corps, First World War

Air Raid Precautions, Second World War

Women's Home Defence

23rd Hussars

22nd Dragoons

12th Lancers

13th Hussars

13th/18th Hussars (three variants)

20th Hussars

5th Dragoon Guards

Above left, right and left:
21st Lancers

10th Imperial Yeomanry　　*North Devon Horse*

Two Members of the Royal Naval Division Wearing Shoulder Titles in Lieu Of Cap Badges

ANSON   *RND*

Above: *ANSON Shoulder title worn as cap badge, as per picture*

Right: *Queen Alexandra's Imperial Nursing Service (Reserve), Cap And Collar Badge*

Tippet Badges
Left: Territorial Force Nursing Service (1908-1920)

Right: Territorial Army Nursing Service (1920-1949)

Queen Alexandra's Imperial Nursing Service (Reserve)

First World War (left) and Second World War (right), Tippet badges

Above left and right: *15th King's Hussars*

Rough Riders

Leicestershire Imperial Yeomanry

Leicestershire Yeomanry

V Force

9th Irish Horse

Royal Monmouth Royal Engineers

Queen's Own Oxfordshire Hussars Yeomanry

Army Ordnance Corps Helmet Plate

Berkshire Imperial Yeomanry

25th Dragoons

4th Prince of Wales' Own Gurkha Rifles

Above left: *4th Queen's Own Hussars*

Above middle: *7th Hussars*

Above right: *23rd County Of London Yeomanry (Sharpshooters), Armoured Car Company*

Central India Horse

24th Lancers

Surrey Yeomanry

Guards Machine Gun Regiment

Guards Machine Gun Battalion

Corps of Military Accountants

South London Volunteer Training Corps (This badge was used by many units, only the name on the scroll changed)

Control Commission Germany

Corps of Military Police

Royal Military Police

Gurkha Military Police

Military Provost Staff Corps,
First World War

Royal Military Academy, Sandhurst

Royal Horse Artillery,
George VI monogram, which
changed with the monarch
from Edward VII to date.

Chapter 19

LIONS

Above left and right: *1st Royal Devon Hussars Yeomanry*

Staff Officer Appointment

Herefordshire Regiment, 1908-1947

Herefordshire Light Infantry, 1947

Duke of Wellington's Regiment, West Riding

Above left and right: *Loyal North Lancashire*

7th Dragoon Guards

The King's Own

King's Own Royal Border Regiment

Lancastrian Brigade, 1958

15th King's Hussars

Above left and right: *Royal Army Pay Corps*

Ayrshire Yeomanry

Infantry Training Battalions

The Royal Dragoons

Military Foot Police

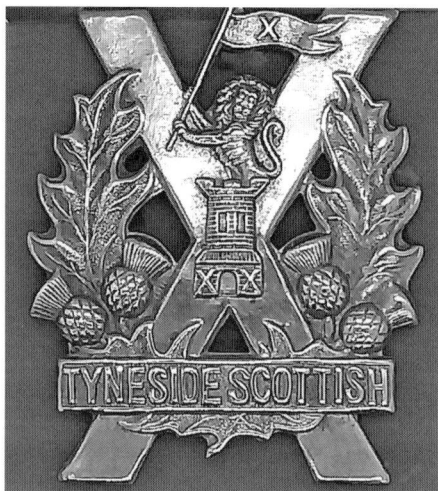

Tyneside Scottish, 1916 Pattern

Women's Royal Army Corps,
1949-1992

Queen Victoria's School

14th (County of London) Battalion,
London Scottish

Chapter 20

NUMBERS

As discussed elsewhere in this book, regiments had a number as well as a name, and most were known by their numbers.

Only a few examples of numbers are shown here as it would be silly to list them all numerically when a simple example or two of one form of badge would suffice. This book would be hundreds of pages long, and that is not the purpose, it is an aid to identifying badges and not to list all badges.

Pictured below are officers of the 48th of Foot. Other officers of this period had the same form of hat and jacket, but with their regiments numbers on the front (it is called uniform for a reason).

This is the same as the Glengarry badges where, at one point, numbers were used. In others, regimental devices were used, such as the castle for the Northamptonshires.

Above is another example, this time from the 54th of Foot.

The Heroes of Lucknow

Surviving uninjured officers, senior non-commissioned officers and other ranks of the 32nd Foot (later The Duke of Cornwall's Light

Infantry) from the siege of Lucknow during the Great Mutiny of 1857 in India. Interesting variations on hats can be seen, as well as the very clear 32, which is visible on the majority of them. Also note the bugle horn above the numbers. It is also to be noted that the Good Conduct Chevrons are on the lower right arm prior to their move to the lower left arm. It appears that they have been issued their Indian Mutiny medals, and family member Henry Adolphus Brett is the scowling corporal middle rear with arms folded, just so we can see his chevrons clearly. The central chap with the different coloured jacket is a drummer. The officer front right with the sword has a sash across his chest, it is the reverse of the sergeant's sash as it is going left to right.

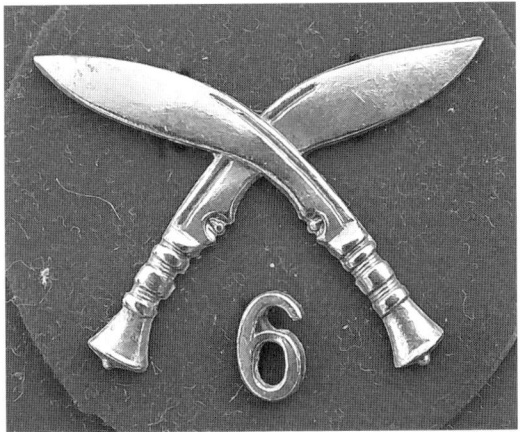

3rd, 5th, 6th and 7th Gurkha Rifles

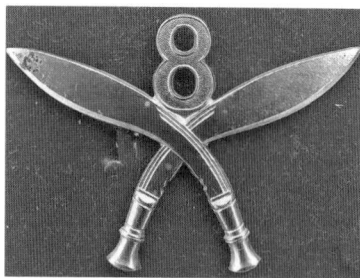

Above left and middle: *8th and 9th Gurkha Rifles*

Above right:*Another style of badge with the regimental device, and a number within the wreath. This is the 64th Regt 2nd Staffordshire (North Stafford)*

Above left, middle and right: *A selection of Infantry Glengarry badges, as described at the beginning of this chapter*

A Shako Plate for the 48th (Northamptonshire) Regiment of Foot. Again, all the line infantry regiments would have this type of badge if they wore the Shako

Above and right: *5th Royal Irish Lancers*

9th Lancers

13th Hussars

16th Lancers

26th Hussars

18th Hussars

25th County of London
Cyclists

7th (City of London)
Battalion, The London
Regiment

Chapter 21

OTHER ANIMALS

Left, below left and below right: *The Queen's Regiment (Royal West Surrey)*

The Manchester Regiment, 1900-1922

The Labour Corps, as well as the Volunteer Training Corps

Westminster Dragoons Yeomanry

General Service Corps, other ranks from 1942 and Officer's General List, First and Second World Wars

Warwickshire and Worcester Yeomanry

Warwickshire Imperial Yeomanry

Warwickshire Yeomanry

Shropshire Yeomanry

4th Battalion Seaforth Highlanders

19th Hussars

British and Asian King's Colonials

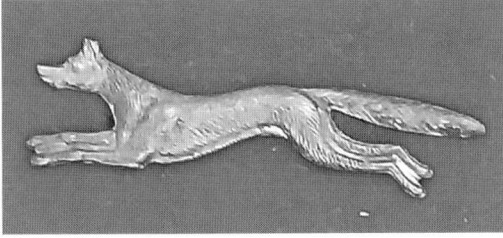

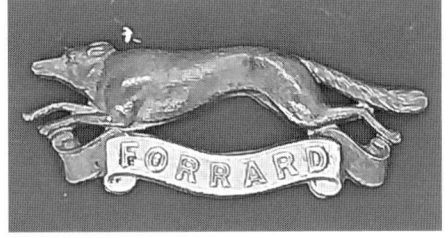

Above left and right: *East Riding (of Yorkshire) Yeomanry variants*

Queen's Own Yeomanry

Royal Dublin Fusiliers

2nd Battalion The Duke Of Wellington's Regiment, 1881-1902

Argyll and Sutherland Highlanders

Royal Munster Fusiliers

British American King's Colonials

*Royal Army Veterinary Corps,
from 1918-Date*

Royal Army Medical Corps

Long Range Desert Group

Chapter 22

OTHER 'THINGS'

This chap wears a button in his cap. It is the Training Reserve, but some state he is also a Kitchener recruit, without an issued badge, and therefore given an extra button to wear.

Training Reserve
Another chap with a 'button' in his cap. The 'Tunic, Simplified' and the 1914 belt would normally point to him being a Kitchener recruit.

Some Kitchener units did have various pin back badges and discs issued in lieu of a badge. This badge, on closer inspection under a magnifying glass, appears not to be the General Service button worn by the Training Reserve, but something else.

Other Things Not Covered

These are the oddities of the British and Empire forces which have not been covered in previous chapters. The Canadian and Australian badges have been added due to the number of them found in family photographs. Many family members emigrated at the end of the 19th century to the Dominions of the Empire, and when the First World War broke out, they found themselves far from home but wishing to defend it. They joined their new country's armies, and the Maple Leaf of Canada (found in flowers and plants), the Rising Sun of Australia, and various fern badges for New Zealand are frequently found.

The open book of learning of the early Army Educational Corps badge (which was replaced by the Torch of Learning in 1946) is included as are the crowns of Howe and Anson battalions of the Royal Naval Division.

The armorial badge of the Honourable Artillery Company is here, along with the Fleur de Lys of the Kings Regiment and the Manchester Regiment.

The Second World War raised Reconnaissance Corps badge with the point of the spear (the sharp end of the army) and two lightning bolts (speed) is here too.

A few badges include a rope knot. These are invariably connected to Staffordshire. The knot device itself is shrouded in mystery. Some say that it comes from an executioner only having one piece of rope to execute three prisoners. Others claim it dates to the year 913 and Ethelfleda, daughter of King Alfred, who used her girdle to symbolically connect the three lands into Staffordshire. There is also a claim that it comes from the arms of the Stafford family themselves and only dates to either 1583 or 1443 depending upon which member of the family used it first.

The 4th and 7th Battalions of the Hampshire Regiment appear to have riding stirrups on their badges. In fact it is the New Forest 'Dog Gauge'. Any dog that could pass through the gauge was allowed into the New Forest. The original is said to have belonged to William II (Rufus) who was shot 'accidentally' in the New Forest on 2 August 1100.

Some of the badges of the battalions from the 63rd Royal Naval Division. These units were initially formed of Royal Navy and Royal Marine Reservists, in addition to volunteers surplus to the fleet requirements in 1914. They served on the Western Front and at Gallipoli. Each battalion was given the name of a famous Royal Navy commander. Other badges from the 8 battalions formed can be found elsewhere in this book, the ship and crown ones are here. The Anson badge appears with its collar badge.

Petty Officer of the Royal Navy

Royal Navy Petty Officer

Honourable Artillery Company Beret badge, post 1953

Australian Commonwealth Military Forces

Dublin County Militia

South Mayo Militia

17th Lancers also 17th/21st Lancers

Army Educational Corps (left), Royal Army Educational Corps (centre and right)

Jewish Battalions of The Royal Fusiliers

No 1 Demolition Squadron, 'Popski's Private Army'

Parachute Regiment

Special Air Service

11th Hussars

Leicestershire Yeomanry

4th Volunteer Battalion Hampshire Regiment

7th Battalion Hampshire Regiment

Above left and right: *Reconnaissance Corps (two variants)*

Royal Armoured Corps, 2nd Pattern

Royal Pioneer Corps, 1st Pattern

Royal Army Medical Corps, 1st Pattern

North Staffordshire Regiment

64th Foot 2nd Staffords (North Stafford)

Stafford Volunteer Rifles

South Staffordshire Regiment

Staffordshire Yeomanry, Victorian

Staffordshire Yeomanry, 1902-1953

Rutland Home Guard, Second World War

Upper Thames Patrol, Home Guard, Second World War

Isle of Man Home Guard, 1952

Royal Gloucestershire Hussars Yeomanry

Westminster Dragoons Yeomanry

Cheshire Railway Volunteers

Women's Home Defence

Female Munitions Workers, First World War

Women's Land Army, First World War

Manchester Regiment, post 1923

7th Battalion Manchester Regiment, post 1923

King's Regiment (Manchester and Liverpool), 1958

New Zealand Expeditionary Force, 1914-1915

Home Counties Brigade, 1958

Chapter 23

SPHINX

A member of a Territorial
Force Band of the
Lincolnshire Regiment,
1908-1912

The Lincolnshire Regiment, 1900-1946

Territorial Battalions of the
Lincolnshire Regiment, 1908-1946

The Royal Lincolnshire Regiment, 1946-1958

The Lincolnshire Regiment Officers,
1900-1946

The Gloucestershire Regiment

Territorial Battalions of the Gloucestershire
Regiment

The Royal Gloucestershire, Berkshire
and Wiltshire Regiment, 1994-2007

Badge worn on rear of hat for the
Gloucestershire Regiment and
Descendant Battalions

South Lancashire Regiment

South Wales Borderers

The Essex Regiment

The Dorsetshire Regiment, post 1900

The Dorsetshire Regiment, pre 1900

The Devon and Dorset Regiment

The East Lancashire Regiment

Chapter 24

STAGS OR DEER

Above left and right: *Seaforth Highlanders (subject is Lieutenant R.A.W. Hunter)*

Gordon Highlanders

Lovat's Scouts

Highland Brigade, 1958

Royal Warwickshire Regiment

Huntingdonshire Cyclists, 1914-1920
(5th Battalion Northamptonshire
Regiment thereafter) and Huntingdonshire
Home Guard, 1940-1944

Hertfordshire Militia, Victorian

Hertfordshire Regiment

Hertfordshire Yeomanry

Hertfordshire Yeomanry

1st Hertfordshire Rifle Volunteers

Bedfordshire Glengarry
Badge, Victorian

Bedfordshire Regiment Helmet
Plate Centre

Bedfordshire Regiment,
pre 1900

Bedfordshire Regiment, 1900-1919

Bedfordshire and Hertfordshire Regiment,
1919-1958

Chapter 25

STARS

Above left and right: *Army Service Corps.*

The 1855-1861 Shako Star

48th Foot

35th Foot

The Home Service Helmet Plate

Medical Staff Corps

Northamptonshire Regiment

Middlesex Regiment

Norfolk Regiment

Royal Anglian Regiment, Band and Drums

Army Service Corps, Victorian

Army Service Corps, 1902-1918

A Second World War Officer of the Royal Army Service Corps

Royal Army Service Corps, 1918-1965

Gurkha Transport Regiment

Indian Supply And Transport Corps

Royal Corps Of Transport, 1965-1993

Royal Logistic Corps, 1993-Date

Cheshire Regiment, Victorian

Cheshire Regiment, 1900-1922

Cheshire Regiment, 1922-2007

Above left, middle and right: *Devonshire Regiment*

1st King's Dragoon Guards, 1915-1937

North Somerset Yeomanry

1st Hertfordshire Rifle Volunteers,
Victorian

4th Royal Irish Dragoon Guards

Worcestershire Regiment, 1900-1925

Above left, middle and right: *The Bedfordshire Regiment. In 1919 the badge changed to the middle version, due to the number of Hertfordshire men who had served with the regiment in the First World War. This badge then remained until 1958.*

Above left and right: Border Regiment Territorial variations, Cumberland and Westmoreland

The Border Regiment   *East Yorkshire Regiment*   *East Surrey Regiment*

23rd Battalion County of London
Regiment

13th Battalion East Surrey, Wandsworth
Battalion, First World War

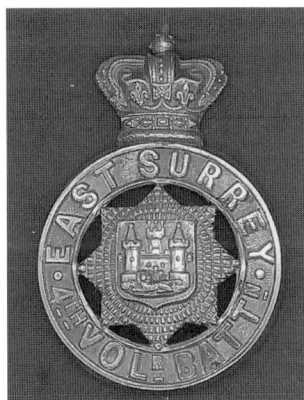

4th Volunteer Battalion, East
Surrey Regiment, Victorian

10th (County of London) Battalion,
Hackney Rifles

Above left and right: Royal Sussex Regiment.

Above left and right: *The Cameronians*

1st Battalion Cameronians Pipers, 1921-1968

3rd Norfolk Rifle Volunteer Corps, Victorian

Royal Scots

Scots Guards

2nd Volunteer Battalion
Highland Light Infantry

Highland Light Infantry

Highland Cyclist Battalion

92nd Gordon Highlanders Victorian

The Black Watch (Royal
Highlanders)

East Anglian Brigade, 1958

Royal Anglian Regiment, 1964-Date

Royal Anglian Regiment (top), East Anglian Brigade/Regiment (bottom), for size comparison

Above left and right: *The music hall star, Vesta Tilley, wearing the uniform of an officer of the Lincolnshire Regiment. You can see the Lincolnshire Regiment badge on 'her' cap and here.*

Above left and right: The Coldstream Guards

Middlesex Volunteer Regiment, Victorian

Guards Machine Gun Battalion Officers, First World War

Irish Guards

Middlesex Yeomanry, George VI

Middlesex Imperial Yeomanry, Edward VII

Royal Dragoon Guards, 1992-Date

Above left and right: *Helmet Plate Stars of the Royal Marines*

Hampshire Regiment Officers, pre-1947

2nd Hampshire Rifle Volunteers Victorian

Worcestershire Regiment, 1925-1958 and 1969-1970

Royal Hampshire and Gloucestershire Regiment (made but never issued)

Worcestershire Regiment Glengarry Badge, 1871-1895

Royal Army Chaplains Department (Jewish)

Chapter 26

STICKS, RIFLES AND LANCES

Above left and right: *5th Royal Irish Lancers*

3rd Carabiniers

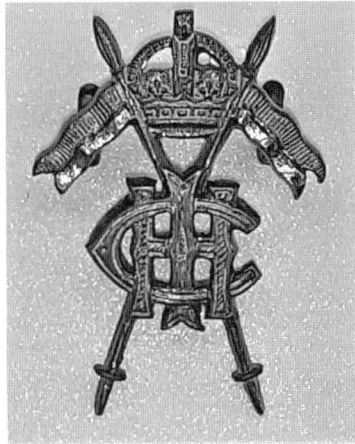

Central India Horse

6th Dragoon Guards

Hampshire Carabiniers

9th Lancers

12th Lancers

16th Lancers

24th Lancers

Above left, middle and right: *Three variations on the 21st Lancers*

27th Lancers

25th Dragoons

Women's Home Defence

Small Arms School Corps

South London Volunteer Training Corps (This badge was used by many units, only the name on the scroll changed)

23rd (County of London) Yeomanry 'Sharpshooters', Armoured Car Company

Above and below: *3rd (County of London) 'Sharpshooters' variants*

Chapter 27

TANKS

Tank Corps, First World War

1st Armoured Motor Battery, Mesopotamia, First World War

Royal Tank Corps, 1924 (withdrawn same year)

Left: *Royal Tank Corps, circa 1930.*

Right: *Royal Tank Corps, 1924-1939 and Royal Tank Regiment, 1939-Date*

Chapter 28

TIGERS

Left and below: *The Leicestershire Regiment (Territorials)*

The Leicestershire Regiment, 1900-1946

Territorial Battalions of the Leicestershire Regiment

Uppingham School OTC and CCF

Royal Leicestershire Regiment, 1946-1964

Royal Dublin Fusiliers

Royal Munster Fusiliers

The Hampshire Regiment, 1900-1946

The Royal Hampshire Regiment, 1946-1992

The York and Lancaster Regiment

Chapter 29

WHEELS

*An Officer of the Army Cyclist Corps,
First World War*

Army Cyclist Corps

City of London Cyclist Battalion

Hampshire Cyclist Battalion

Northern Cyclist Battalion

25th County of London Cyclists

Above left: *City of London Cyclist Battalion*

Above right: *National Motor Volunteers, First World War*

Chapter 30

WOMEN'S SERVICES

Two members of the WAAC with three VADS, First World War

Women's Army Auxiliary Corps, First World War

Queen Mary's Army Auxiliary Corps, First World War

Queen Alexandra's Imperial Military Nursing Service, 1902-1949

Queen Alexandra's Imperial Military Nursing Service (Reserve), 1908-1949

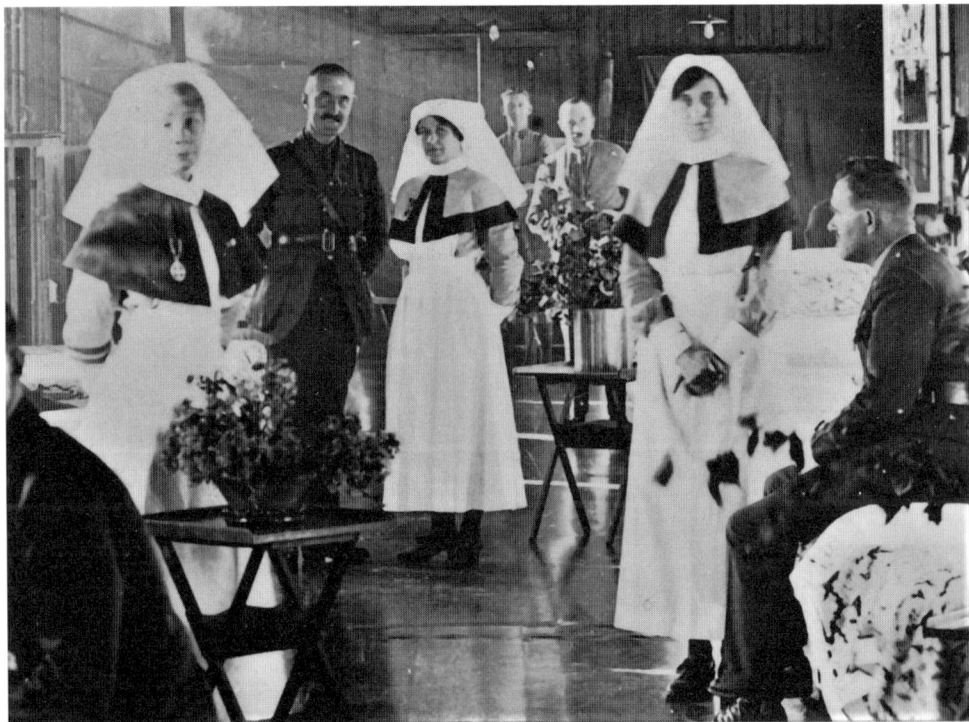

Right: *Territorial Army Nursing Service, 1920-1949 (Territorial Force Nursing Service)*

Below left: *Queen Alexandra's Royal Army Nursing Corps, 1949-1952*

Below right: *Queen Alexandra's Royal Army Nursing Corps, 1952-Date*

Army Nursing Tippet Badges

Princess Christian's Army Nursing Reserve, 2nd Boer War

Above left and right: *Queen Alexandra's Imperial Military Nursing Service (Reserve). Smaller Tippet badge is from the Second World War, whilst the larger one and the one in the photo of the nurse is from the First World War*

Territorial Force Nursing Service (left) and Territorial Army Nursing Service (right)

Queen Alexandra's Imperial Military Nursing Service

QAIMNS in walking out dress, 1936. Note the collar badges

Right: *Territorial Force Nursing Service. Note the Tippet badge on the two seated nurses.*

Below: *QAIMNS, tropical wear 'Whites', Second World War*

Above left and right: *British Red Cross Society*

First Aid Nursing Yeomanry (FANY)

Above left and right: *Initially a private organisation which did not contain trained nurses, they were eventually accepted by the Belgian government to lend aid in 1915. They never used horses outside of Great Britain. In the Second World War they became more military and counted many female SOE agents amongst their ranks. They are now known as the Princess Royal's Volunteer Corps*

Army Service Corps. Worn by female drivers in the First World War

The Women's Legion, First World War

Above left and right: *First World War Munitionette and badge*

Above left and right: *Women's Land Army, First World War*

Women's Land Army,
Second World War

The woman below left is the great Music Hall artiste, Vesta Tilley. She is dressed as an officer of the Lincolnshire Regiment. The young lady bottom right is wearing her chap's Service Dress cap and greatcoat. There was nothing unusual about this, and many, many examples exist. Though the exchange of clothing in the top right image is quite unusual!

Whilst women in the First World War did not serve in front line positions, they did contribute to the war effort by joining the Women's Army Auxiliary Corps (WAAC), Queen Mary's Army Auxiliary Corps

These pictures show women dressed as men in uniform, and in the case of the upper right, vice versa as well!

(QMAAC), Queen Alexandra's Imperial Military Nursing Service (QAIMNS), etc. Some female motor drivers wore the Army Service Corps (ASC) badge, but not the infantry badge. In the Second World War women were nearer to the front line and served in anti-aircraft batteries as well as in nursing, the Auxiliary Territorial Service (ATS) and the Women's Royal Navy Service (WRNS), amongst others.

Above left and right: *An officer (left) and an aircraftswoman of the Women's Auxiliary Air Force (WAAF)*

Women's Home Defence. Most members joined the Home Guard once women were allowed.

Women's Home Guard Auxiliary

Women's Royal Army Corps,
1949-1992

Auxiliary Territorial Service, 1938-1949
Army

Above left and right: *Army Remount Services. Although rarer than some of the other badges worn by women, these were worn in the First World War*

Chapter 31

WREATHS

A Kitchener Volunteer of the Middlesex Regiment

Middlesex Regiment, Regular Battalions

Middlesex Regiment, 10th Battalion Territorials

Middlesex Regiment, 17th Battalion Footballers

Middlesex Regiment, Cadets

Above left and right: *Cameron Highlanders*

Liverpool Scottish, post 1937

Royal Scots Fusiliers Pipers

4th Volunteer Battalion
Gordon Highlanders

The Cameronians

Liverpool Scottish
1908-1937

Gordon Highlanders

Argyll And Sutherland Highlanders

King's Own Scottish Borderers

Scottish Horse 2nd Pattern, 1903

Scottish Horse 1st Pattern, 1900

14th (County of London) London Scottish

Tyneside Scottish, 1916 pattern

Corps of Royal Engineers

Queen Victoria Royal Engineers

Edward VII Royal Engineers

George V Royal Engineers

Edward VIII Royal Engineers

Queen Elizabeth II Royal Engineers

Badges that are often confused with Royal Engineers badges:

Queen's Own Dorset Yeomanry

British West Indies Regiment (Caribbean Volunteers, First World War)

10th (County Of London) Paddington Rifles

King's Own Malta Regiment

*17th County of London Battalion
(Poplar and Stepney Rifles) pre 1926*

Royal Greenjackets

*19th County of London Battalion
(St Pancras)*

*8th City of London Battalion Post
Office Rifles*

*7th (Robin Hood's) Battalion
Sherwood Foresters*

*18th Middlesex Rifle Volunteers
(London Irish), pre 1901*

The Rifle Brigade, 1903-10

The Rifle Brigade, 1910-36

Above left: *The Rifle Brigade, 1937-56*

Above right: *The Rifle Brigade, 19th Battalion*

Left: *The Rifle Brigade, 1956-58*

Above left, middle and right: *7th and 8th Battalions West Yorkshire, Leeds Rifles*

Above left and right: *The Border Regiment, officers variants*

Radnor Home Guard, 1952

Forester Brigade, 1958

Royal Army Chaplains Department:

Christian

Jewish

South Lancashire Regiment

South Wales Borderers

Army Air Corps, 1942-50

Army Air Corps, 1957-Date

Badge worn on rear of hat by the
Gloucestershire Regiment and descendants

25th (County of London) Cyclists

Above left and right: *18th Hussars*

18th Hussars

13th Hussars

Northamptonshire Collar Badge. Used on field service cap

Dorsetshire Regiment

Essex Regiment

Northamptonshire Regiment, post 1900

Suffolk Regiment

Northamptonshire Volunteer Training Corps

Dorsetshire Regiment, Pre 1900

City of London Yeomanry

8th Battalion Hampshire Regiment,
Isle of Wight Rifles

Royal Observer Corps

Women's Legion

Norfolk Regiment

2nd Battalion Monmouthshire Regiment

Warwickshire and Worcestershire Yeomanry

Tank Corps, First World War

Royal Tank Corps, 1924 (withdrawn same year)

Royal Tank Corps, 1924-1939, Royal Tank Regiment, 1939-Date

1st Armoured Motor Battery, Mesopotamia, First World War

United Nations Peacekeeping: Other Ranks
Enamelled Badge

United Nations Peacekeeping: Officer's
Embroidered Badge

1869-1878 Shako Plate. These are all the
same but the centre badge/number is different

1st Sussex Rifle Volunteer Corps

Leicester Imperial Yeomanry

Leicester Yeomanry

Royal Flying Corps, 1912-1918

Royal Air Force, 1918-Date

*Military Provost Staff Corps,
First World War*

Control Commission Germany

*Women's Army Auxiliary Corps,
First World War*

*Queen Mary's Army Auxiliary Corps,
First World War*

Auxiliary Territorial Service, 1938-1949

Army Veterinary Department, 1902-1906

Army Veterinary Corps, 1903-1918

Royal Army Veterinary Corps, 1918-Date

Army Dental Corps, 1921-1946

Royal Army Dental Corps, 1946-Date

Queen's Bays

Royal Armoured Corps 1st Pattern

Women's Royal Army Corps, 1949-1992

York and Lancaster Regiment

King's Own Royal Border Regiment

Hampshire Regiment, 1900-1946

*Royal Hampshire Regiment,
1946-1992*

Queen Victoria School

Royal Pioneer Corps, 2nd Pattern   *Small Arms School Corps*

*South London Volunteer Training Corps.
(This badge was used by many units,
only the name on the scroll changed)*

*Corps of Military Police, First World
War*

Royal Military Police

Gurkha Military Police

Lancastrian Brigade, 1958

Above left, middle and right: *London Rifle Brigade variants*

8th Scottish Volunteer Battalion, The King's Liverpool Regiment, 1902-1908

4th Volunteer Battalion, Hampshire Regiment

7th Battalion Hampshire Regiment

Royal Army Medical Corps, 1902-1953, (1953 – Date with Queen's Crown)

Drake Battalion, Royal Naval Division, First World War

6th Battalion Hampshire Regiment

East Lancashire Regiment

3rd Volunteer Battalion, Hampshire Regiment

Duke of Lancaster's Own Yeomanry

Intelligence Corps

Worcestershire Hussars Yeomanry

Westmorland and Cumberland Yeomanry

64th Foot, 2nd Staffordshire (North Staffords)

Royal Marine Light Infantry

Royal Marine Artillery

Above left and right: *Royal Marine Band Service*

King Edward's Horse

King Edward's Horse

Lincolnshire Yeomanry

Legion of Frontiersmen

Inns of Court OTC; Inns of Court Regiment; Inns of Court and County Yeomanry

Royal Irish Rifles Pipers, 1902-1922

8th Irish Battalion, King's Liverpool Regiment

WHERE TO GO NEXT AND FURTHER RESEARCH

Birth, marriage and death certificates
These are very important to ensure you have the right person. They also provide occupations and, often, a regimental/service number on the wedding certificate and the birth certificates of any children.

Absent voters list
Available from 1918 but not often available online. You will need to go to the County Record Office of where the person was living at the time of enlistment. It will give name, regiment and regimental number.

1939 Register
This is not a census, it is a register for all those who were living in 1939 for the purpose of National Service and for the issue of Identity Cards and, later, the NHS. It was kept up to date until 1991, so you can find maiden and married names for women. The census of 1931 was lost in a fire, and the 1941 census was not taken, so this is an important snapshot of British life from 1921-1951.

Newspaper archives
Some of these are online, but not all. It is best to look in your County Record Office for copies. Many named photographs of First World War soldiers appeared in the newspapers, especially the local ones. Sometimes notices of requests for information on missing soldiers appeared in the national press. These often carried a photograph too.

The London Gazette
The official journal of the government. Military and civil awards can be found therein, as well as officers' commissions and dates of promotion.

Their website has, in the past, been an absolute minefield to navigate. They have now added a First World War section. It can be useful if you can find who it is you are looking for, or know the dates, especially as officers in the First World War did not have numbers. Other than that, it is a laborious, time-consuming research tool that could be much better and more user friendly. Printed army lists are much easier to use.

International Committee Red Cross Geneva PoW records
First and Second World War Prisoner of War records are held by the Red Cross.

For Second World War records: https://www.icrc.org/en/document/request-information-about-individuals-detained-during-second-world-war-or-spanish-civil-war-quota

For First World War records: https://grandeguerre.icrc.org/

Army Lists
These are monthly, quarterly and yearly returns published variously over the years by the War Office, General Hart and the MOD. These have what the *London Gazette Online* makes difficult to find: officers' commissions, promotions, regiments, and post-1921 service numbers. They can be found online, but I always prefer looking through a physical copy, as it is, again, so much easier to navigate.

https://digital.nls.uk/british-military-lists/archive/88735803

Services of Military Officers
The 1920 edition of this tome has all the officers, and those of officer status (QAIMNS, TFNS, etc) who were still serving or were on the Retired List as of this date. A mine of information if researching an officer.

Ancestry/Find My Past
These can be very useful, especially for pre-1913 service (WO97), and service in the First WorldWar. Beware though, Ancestry has a lot of military records hidden behind a secondary pay wall called Fold3. This is an American serviceman's site which is now being filled with British Military information. You can access some of it for free if you are a member of the Western Front Association

I was lucky enough to have been given some photos of First World War Soldiers by a family member. They had written on the back who they thought the subject was but this was done without any recourse to research. Luckily the cap badges were visible and I remembered the subjects from my childhood. They were, in fact, two different brothers-in-law of the person named on the rear. This was confirmed by the grandson of one of them and these pictures appear in this book.

Medal Index Cards

Medal Index Cards (MIC). These list all of those entitled to medals from the First World War. Sadly, if your relative did not have an entitlement, there will be no MIC but if they had such entitlement they can be of great use. Look initially on the National Archives website as the basic information on there is free but beware as a soldier in the First World War could have more than one number, and more than one regiment in which they served. I have seen up to FOUR of each on a card in the past.

Soldiers' effects

These can be found on Ancestry, which shows where a soldier's personal items were sent and to whom. Very useful.

First World War and earlier pension records

Some are available online. 19th century records are held at the National Archives (I found one for a soldier of the Peninsular War under Wellington). *https://www.nationalarchives.gov.uk/help-with-your-research/research-guides/ disability-dependants-pensions-first-world-war/*

MOD for ANY post-1921 service

All military service post-1921 is held by the Ministry of Defence (MOD) only. It is not available online. You may find a snippet, such as the Royal Artillery Tracer Cards, but if you want service details, you will have to go to the MOD. Some sites may appear to have records after this date but they do not. Avoid them. www.gov.uk/guidance/request-records-of-deceased-service-personnel

National Archives

If you have the time, visit the National Archives. You can dig through all sorts of records here and it is especially important for 19th century military records.

Scotland's People

A useful site if your ancestor lived in, or came from, there.

Family ephemera

If you are lucky, one of your family may have been a hoarder of old documents. My parents were and I found, or was given, a pile of birth certificates, death certificates, military documents, Women's Land Army paperwork amongst other things. Dig through and attach them to the right person on your tree but beware...

Family stories are like a game of 'Chinese Whispers'.

Is it 'send reinforcements, we are going to advance' or 'send three and fourpence, we are going to a dance'? Family stories get handed down, and whilst there may be some elements of truth to them, do not take them as facts. As with everything else in any form of historical research, make sure to prove your 'facts', and in family history, prove them from at least two written or photographic sources. One place to find information is the rim or rear of medals. It was only for the Second World War that medals were not all named and numbered, along with the name of (at least one!) their unit.

British Red Cross VAD

A little known database of records is held by the British Red Cross Society from the First World War. Any volunteer medical personnel were recruited through the Voluntary Aid Detachment scheme. This is a really useful site for researching them. It also includes the Friends' Ambulance Service, the Quaker pacifists who served as non combatants. https://vad.redcross.org.uk

First World War voice recordings

https://sounds.bl.uk/Accents-and-dialects/Berliner-Lautarchiv-British-and-Commonwealth-recordings

If your ancestor was taken prisoner by the Germans during the First World War, you may be lucky enough to be able to hear his voice. These are recordings made by the Germans of British and Empire PoWs between 1915 and 1918, and is also a valuable resource for the accents and dialects of the time.

Commonwealth War Graves Commission

I have saved this until last. You may well have heard of them. The CWGC looks after, in perpetuity, the graves of those lost in both the First and Second World Wars. Actually some graves are not in the records; these are being researched by a group called 'In From the Cold'. They also have a list of private memorials in Great Britain to those who died at home and were given headstones by their families. These stones, when they fall into disrepair, are replaced by the CWGC so the memories are continued. The website has the list of all those who died, including British civilian casualties. You can find the location of the memorial or headstone, their unit, date of death, the Regimental or Service number (unless officers in the First World War), and, frequently, the name of the next of kin on the website. https://www.cwgc.org/

ABBREVIATIONS USED

ADC	Army Dental Corps
ASC	Army Service Corps
AVC	Army Veterinary Corps
AVD	Army Veterinary Department
BAOR	British Army Of The Rhine (Occupation force after the First World War, and NATO posting during the Cold War)
BEF	British Expeditionary Force
Coy	Company
CWGC	Commonwealth War Graves Commission
DG	Dragoon Guards
HG	Home Guard
K1-K4	The four armies raised by Kitchener from 1914
KDG	King's Dragoon Guards
MGC	Machine Gun Corps
MMG	Mounted Machine Gun Corps
NATO	North Atlantic Treaty Organisation
OTAN	French abbreviation for NATO
QAIMNS	Queen Alexandra's Imperial Military Nursing Servce
QAIMNS(R)	Queen Alexandra's Imperial Military Nursing Service (Reserve)
RND	Royal Naval Division, First World War
TA	Territorial Army
TANS	Territorial Army Nursing Service
TF	Territorial Force
TFNS	Territorial Force Nursing Service
VAD	Voluntary Aid Detachment (medical)
WHD	Women's Home Defence

CAVALRY, 1881 TO 1922

1st Life Guards
Formed in 1660 by Charles II in Holland

2nd Life Guards
Also formed in 1660 by Charles II. Originally named The Duke of Albemarle's Troop of Guards.

Royal Horse Guards (The Blues)
Originally part of Parliament's New Model Army which were ordered to disband upon the Restoration of Charles II, the guards continued and, in January 1661, became 'The Oxford Blues' after their colonel, the Duke of Oxford.

1st King's Dragoon Guards
One of the many regiments of the British Army raised in 1685 on the accession of James II.

2nd Dragoon Guards (Queen's Bays)
Also raised in 1685 and mounted upon bay-coloured chargers.

3rd (Prince of Wales) Dragoon Guards
Another 1685 regiment.

4th (Royal Irish) Dragoon Guards
1685 regiment, originally 'Arrans Cuirassiers'.

5th (Princess Charlotte of Wales) Dragoon Guards
Raised in 1685 and known originally as 'Seventh Horse'.

6th Dragoon Guards
Originally raised in 1685 as the 'Queen Dowager's Regiment of Horse'. It was given the name 'King's Carabiniers' by William III in 1691, due to their distinguished service and long pistols, which were known as 'Carabines'. This name was later changed to Carbines when short mounted rifles were introduced.

7th (Princess Royal's) Dragoon Guards
Raised in 1688 and known variously as the 'Earl of Devonshire's Horse', 'Schombergs Horse', 'Ligoniers Horse' and then 'The Black Horse', all within the space of their first 100 years!

1st Royal Dragoons
Formed in 1661 to guard Tangier, the dowry bought by Charles II's new wife, the Infanta Catherine of Portugal, upon their marriage.

2nd Dragoons (Royal Scots Greys)
Raised in 1678 and by 1700 they were already known as the 'Grey Dragoons' due to their white horses (white horses are known as 'greys').

3rd (King's Own) Hussars
Another 1685 regiment, originally called 'The Queen Consort's Regiment of Dragoons'.

4th (Queen's Own) Hussars
Formed in 1685 as 'The Princess Anne of Denmark's Regiment of Dragoons'.

5th (Royal Irish) Lancers
Raised as the 'Royal Irish Dragoons' in 1689.

6th (Inniskilling) Dragoons
Formed in 1689 and in 1690, it gained the above title which didn't change throughout its history, until amalgamation.

7th (Queen's Own) Hussars
Raised in 1689 as 'Cunningham's Regiment of Dragoons'.

8th (King's Royal Irish) Hussars
Raised in Ireland in 1693.

9th (Queen's Royal) Lancers
Originally raised in 1697, and then re-embodied in 1715 as 'Wynne's Dragoons'.

10th (Prince of Wales' Own Royal) Hussars
Originally raised in 1697, known in 1783 as 'The Prince of Wales' Light Dragoons'.

11th (Prince Albert's Own) Hussars
Also raised in 1697 and known as the 'Cherrypickers' due to the colour of their trousers. The name was originally coined because of the cherry stains on their trousers gained from awaiting battle in a cherry orchard.

12th (Prince of Wales' Royal) Lancers
Raised in 1715 and were stationed in Ireland for 76 years without a move elsewhere. 'The Supple 12th'.

13th Hussars
Raised in 1715 as 'Munden's Dragoons' and known as 'The Lilywhites' due to their white collars and stripes on trousers.

14th (King's) Hussars
Raised twice, firstly in 1697, and again in 1715. Known as 'The Emperor's Chambermaid' due to a silver trophy captured after the battle of Vittoria in 1813.

15th (The King's) Hussars
Raised in 1759 by the future defender of Gibraltar, Colonel George Elliot.

16th (The Queen's) Lancers
Also raised in 1759, the first British Lancer Regiment to use the lance in action.

17th (Duke of Cambridge's Own) Lancers
Another regiment raised in 1759, who were known as 'The Death or Glory Boys' due to the cap badge being a skull and crossed bones. In medieval times, the skull and two femur bones were all that it was believed necessary to ensure resurrection.

18th (Queen Mary's Own) Hussars
Another 1759 raising which was disbanded in 1821 after distinguished service in the Peninsular War against Napoleon. Resurrected in 1868 as a continued service.

19th (Queen Alexandra's Own Royal) Hussars
Originally raised as the 19th Light Dragoons in 1759 and converted to Hussars in 1807. Disbanded and then resurrected in 1860 from the former

regiment of Bengal European Cavalry of the East India Company, which had been disbanded after 'The Great Mutiny' of 1857.

20th Hussars
Originated in Ireland from the light troop of the 6th Inniskilling Dragoons and formed in 1789 (known as 'The Year of the French' as they had landed in Ireland to foment revolt).

21st (Empress of India's) Lancers
Raised 1760, disbanded 1763. Raised again in 1779 and disbanded the same year. Raised in 1794 and again disbanded. Raised for the final time in 1858 as the 3rd Bengal European Cavalry.

The Royal Regiment of Artillery
Containing the Royal Horse Artillery, the Royal Field Artillery, and the Royal Garrison Artillery.

The Corps of Royal Engineers
1722, the Soldier Artificer Corps, then the Corps of Military Artificers and in 1788 they gained their current name.

Appendix 2

FORMER INFANTRY NUMBERING SYSTEM UP TO 1881 AND SUBSEQUENT TITLES

Until 1881	**1881-1922**
• 1st Foot	Royal Scots
• 2nd Foot	Queens Royal West Surrey
• 3rd Foot	East Kent Regiment The Buffs
• 4th Foot	Kings Own Royal Lancaster Regiment
• 5th Foot	Northumberland Fusiliers
• 6th Foot	The Royal Warwickshire Regiment
• 7th Foot	The Royal Fusiliers (City of London Regiment)
• 8th Foot	Liverpool Regiment
• 9th Foot	Norfolk Regiment
• 10th Foot	Lincolnshire Regiment
• 11th Foot	Devon Regiment
• 12th Foot	Suffolk Regiment
• 13th Foot	Somerset Light Infantry
• 14th Foot	West Yorkshire Regiment
• 15th Foot	East Yorkshire Regiment
• 16th Foot	Bedfordshire Regiment
• 17th Foot	Leicestershire Regiment
• 18th Foot	Royal Irish Regiment
• 19th Foot	Yorkshire Regiment (Alexandra Princess of Wales' Own)
• 20th Foot	Lancashire Fusiliers
• 21st Foot	Royal Scots Fusiliers
• 22nd Foot	Cheshire Regiment
• 23rd Foot	Royal Welsh Fusiliers

- 24th Foot   South Wales Borderers
- 25th Foot   Kings Own Scottish Borderers
- 26th Foot   1st Battalion Scottish Rifles (Cameronians)
- 27th Foot   1st Battalion Royal Inniskilling Fusiliers
- 28th Foot   1st Battalion Gloucestershire Regiment
- 29th Foot   1st Battalion Worcestershire Regiment
- 30th Foot   1st Battalion East Lancashire Regiment
- 31st Foot   1st Battalion East Surrey Regiment
- 32nd Foot   1st Battalion Duke of Cornwall's Light Infantry
- 33rd Foot   1st Battalion West Riding Regiment
              (Duke of Wellington's)
- 34th Foot   1st Battalion Border Regiment
- 35th Foot   1st Battalion Royal Sussex Regiment
- 36th Foot   2nd Battalion Worcestershire Regiment
- 37th Foot   1st Battalion Hampshire Regiment
- 38th Foot   1st Battalion South Staffordshire Regiment
- 39th Foot   1st Battalion Dorsetshire Regiment
- 40th Foot   1st Battalion South Lancashire Regiment
- 41st Foot   1st Battalion Welsh Regiment
- 42nd Foot   1st Battalion Royal Highlanders (Black Watch)
- 43rd Foot   1st Battalion Oxfordshire and Buckinghamshire
              Light Infantry
- 44th Foot   1st Battalion Essex Regiment
- 45th Foot   1st Battalion Nottingham and Derbyshire Regiment
- 46th Foot   2nd Battalion Duke of Cornwall's Light Infantry
- 47th Foot   1st Battalion North Lancashire Regiment
- 48th Foot   1st Battalion Northamptonshire Regiment
- 49th Foot   1st Battalion Royal Berkshire Regiment
- 50th Foot   1st Battalion Royal West Kent Regiment
- 51st Foot   1st Battalion (King's Own) Yorkshire Light Infantry
- 52nd Foot   2nd Battalion Oxfordshire and Buckinghamshire
              Light Infantry
- 53rd Foot   1st Battalion Shropshire Light Infantry
- 54th Foot   2nd Battalion Dorsetshire Regiment
- 55th Foot   2nd Battalion Border Regiment
- 56th Foot   2nd Battalion Essex Regiment
- 57th foot   1st Battalion Middlesex Regiment
- 58th Foot   2nd Battalion Northamptonshire Regiment
- 59th foot   2nd Battalion East Lancashire Regiment
- 60th Foot   King's Royal Rifle Corps
- 61st Foot   2nd Battalion Gloucestershire Regiment
- 62nd Foot   1st Battalion Wiltshire Regiment

- 63rd Foot   1st Battalion Manchester Regiment
- 64th Foot   1st Battalion North Staffordshire Regiment
- 65th Foot   1st Battalion York and Lancaster Regiment
- 66th Foot   2nd Battalion Royal Berkshire Regiment
- 67th Foot   2nd Battalion Hampshire Regiment
- 68th Foot   1st Battalion Durham Light Infantry
- 69th Foot   2nd Battalion Welsh Regiment
- 70th Foot   2nd Battalion East Surrey Regiment
- 71st Foot   1st Battalion Highland Light Infantry
- 72nd Foot   1st Battalion Seaforth Highlanders
- 73rd Foot   2nd Battalion Royal Highlanders (Black Watch)
- 74th Foot   2nd Battalion Highland Light Infantry
- 75th Foot   1st Battalion Gordon Highlanders
- 76th Foot   2nd Battalion West Riding Regiment
               (Duke of Wellington's)
- 77th Foot   2nd Battalion Middlesex Regiment
- 78th Foot   2nd Battalion Seaforth Highlanders
- 79th Foot   1st Battalion Cameron Highlanders
- 80th Foot   2nd Battalion South Staffordshire Regiment
- 81st Foot   2nd Battalion North Lancashire Regiment
- 82nd Foot   2nd Battalion South Lancashire Regiment
- 83rd Foot   1st Battalion Royal Irish Rifles
- 84th Foot   2nd Battalion York and Lancaster Regiment
- 85th Foot   2nd Battalion Shropshire Light Infantry
- 86th Foot   2nd Battalion Royal Irish Rifles
- 87th Foot   1st Battalion Royal Irish Fusiliers
- 88th Foot   1st Battalion Connaught Rangers
- 89th Foot   2nd Battalion Royal Irish Fusiliers
- 90th Foot   2nd Battalion Scottish Rifles (Cameronians)
- 91st Foot   1st Battalion Argyll and Sutherland Highlanders
- 92nd Foot   2nd Battalion Gordon Highlanders
- 93rd Foot   2nd Battalion Argyll and Sutherland Highlanders
- 94th Foot   2nd Battalion Connaught Rangers
- 95th Foot   2nd Battalion Nottinghamshire and
               Derbyshire Regiment
- 96th Foot   2nd Battalion Manchester Regiment
- 97th Foot   2nd Battalion Royal West Kent Regiment
- 98th Foot   2nd Battalion North Staffordshire Regiment
- 99th Foot   2nd Battalion Wiltshire Regiment
- 100th Foot   1st Battalion Leinster Regiment
- 101st Foot   1st Battalion Royal Munster Fusiliers
- 102nd Foot   1st Battalion Royal Dublin Fusiliers

- 103rd Foot   2nd Battalion Royal Dublin Fusiliers
- 104th Foot   2nd Battalion Royal Munster Fusiliers
- 105th Foot   2nd Battalion Yorkshire Light Infantry
- 106th Foot   2nd Battalion Durham Light Infantry
- 107th Foot   2nd Battalion Royal Sussex Regiment
- 108th Foot   2nd Battalion Royal Inniskilling Fusiliers
- 109th Foot   2nd Battalion Leinster Regiment
- The Rifle Brigade

Separate to the line infantry are the Foot Guards of the Household Division. These regiments did not have a number and have always been set apart:

- The Grenadier Guards
- The Coldstream Guards
- The Scots Guards
- The Irish Guards
- The Welsh Guards

Appendix 3

THE CURRENT ORDER OF PRECEDENCE

as of 2020

- Household Cavalry
- Royal Horse Artillery
- Royal Armoured Corps
- Royal Regiment of Artillery
- Corps of Royal Engineers
- Royal Corps of Signals
- Infantry
  - Foot Guards
  - Line Infantry
  - The Rifles
- Special Air Service
- Army Air Corps
- Special Reconnaissance Regiment
- Royal Army Chaplains Department
- Royal Logistic Corps
- Royal Army Medical Corps
- Royal Electrical and Mechanical Engineers
- Adjutant General's Corps
- Royal Army Veterinary Corps
- Small Arms School Corps
- Royal Army Dental Corps
- Intelligence Corps
- Royal Army Physical Training Corps
- General Service Corps

- Queen Alexandra's Royal Army Nursing Corps
- Corps of Army Music
- Royal Monmouth Royal Engineers (Militia) (Army Reserve)
- Honourable Artillery Company (Although Army Reserve Regiments, they are included in the order of arms Regular Army)
- Remainder of the Reserve
- Royal Gibraltar Regiment
- Royal Bermuda Regiment

Appendix 4

'LOST' CORPS

- Royal Army Service Corps
- Royal Corps of Transport
- Royal Army Ordnance Corps
- Royal Pioneer Corps
- Army Catering Corps

The above were amalgamated into the Royal Logistic Corps, which for obvious reasons, is known in the army as the 'Really Large Corps'.

The Adjutant General's Corps was formed in 1992 from:

- Royal Army Pay Corps
- The Corps of Royal Military Police
- Military Provost Staff Corps
- Royal Army Educational Corps
- The Army Legal Corps
- Staff Clerks from all other arms and services
- In 1997 the new Military Provost Guard Service was added

Royal Flying Corps
Formed in 1912 and amalgamated on 1 April 1918 with the Royal Naval Air Service to form the Royal Air Force, the world's first independent military air arm

Appendix 5

SOME PREVIOUS LOST UNITS

- Women's Royal Army Corps
- Women's Army Auxiliary Corps
- Queen Mary's Army Auxiliary Corps
- Mobile Defence Corps
- The Home Guard
- Control Commission Germany
- Junior Leaders Battalion
- Army Remounts
- Long Range Desert Group
- Reconnaissance Corps
- Raiding Support Regiment
- The Royal Naval Division
- Machine Gun Corps
- Auxiliary Territorial Service
- School of Musketry
- Army Cyclist Corps

LOST IRISH REGIMENTS
Connaught Rangers
1793-1922
Raised in Connaught in 1793, bearing the name throughout its history

The Leinster Regiment (Prince of Wales)
1858-1922
Raised in Canada.

The Royal Munster Fusiliers
1756-1922
Raised in India in 1756 as the Bengal European Regiment

The Royal Dublin Fusiliers
1748-1922
The two battalions had already accrued, by 1870, 432 years' service in India between them.

Appendix 6

MODERN REGIMENTS, FORMATION DATES, AND THEIR ANTECEDENTS

as of 2020

HOUSEHOLD CAVALRY
The Life Guards
Formed in 1922 on the amalgamation of the 1st and 2nd Life Guards

The Blues and Royals
Formed in 1969 from the Royal Horse Guards and the 1st Dragoons

ROYAL ARMOURED CORPS
1st Queens Dragoon Guards
Formed 1959 from the 1st and 2nd Dragoon Guards.

The Royal Scots Dragoon Guards
Formed in 1971 with the 3rd Dragoon Guards, the 6th Dragoon Guards and the 2nd Dragoons.

The Royal Dragoon Guards
Formed in 1992 with the 4th Dragoon Guards, 5th Dragoon Guards 7th Dragoon Guards and the 6th Dragoons.

THE LIGHT CAVALRY
The Queens Royal Hussars
Formed in 1993 with the 3rd Hussars, the 4th Hussars, the 7th Hussars and the 8th Hussars.

The Royal Lancers
Formed in 2015 with the 5th Lancers, 9th Lancers, 12th Lancers 16th Lancers, 17th Lancers, and the 21st Lancers.

The King's Royal Hussars
Formed in 1992 with the 10th Hussars, 11th Hussars, 14th Hussars and the 20th Hussars.

The Light Dragoons
Formed 1992 with the 13th Hussars, 15th Hussars, 18th Hussars and the 19th Hussars.

The Royal Tank Regiment
Formed in 1992 from the 1st, 2nd, 3rd, 4th, 5th, 6th, 7th and 8th Royal Tank Regiments.

NB
Most of the cavalry regiments had been amalgamated at least once since 1922, and the full list of those antecedent regiments is included for completeness sake.

Appendix 7

INFANTRY AND INFANTRY OF THE LINE

FOOT GUARDS
Grenadier Guards
Formed 1656 as the Royal Regiment of Guards, and the King's Royal Regiment of Guards.

Coldstream Guards
Formed 1650, but as Parliamentary Forces during the Commonwealth, they forfeit their initial service.

Scots Guards
Formed 1642 as the Marquis of Argyll's Regiment.

Irish Guards
Formed 1900.

Welsh Guards
Formed 1915.

INFANTRY OF THE LINE, 2020
The Royal Regiment of Scotland
Formed in 2006 and contains the 1st, 21st, 25th, 42nd, 71st, 73rd, 74th, 75th, 78th, 79th, 91st, 92nd, and 93rd Foot.

The Princess of Wales' Royal Regiment
Formed in 1992 and contains the 2nd, 3rd, 31st, 35th, 37th, 50th, 57th, 67th, 70th, 77th, 97th, and 107th Foot.

The Duke of Lancaster's Regiment
Formed in 2006 and contains the 4th, 8th, 30th 34th, 40th, 47th, 55th, 59th, 63rd, 81st, 82nd and the 96th of Foot.

The Royal Regiment of Fusiliers
Formed in 1968 and contains the 5th, 6th, 7th, and 20th Foot.

The Royal Anglian Regiment
Formed originally in 1958 as the East Anglian Brigade, renamed East Anglian Regiment in 1960, and the Royal Anglian Regiment in 1964 and contains the 9th, 10th 12th, 16th, 17th, 44th, 48th, 56th and 58th of Foot.

The Yorkshire Regiment
Formed in 2006 and contains 14th, 15th, 19th, 33rd, and 76th of Foot.

The Mercian Regiment
Formed in 2007 and contains 22nd, 29th, 36th, 38th, 45th, 64th, 80th, 95th, and 98th of Foot.

The Royal Welsh Regiment
Formed in 2006 and contains 23rd, 24th, 41st, and 69th of Foot.

The Royal Irish Regiment
Formed in 1992 and contains 27th, 83rd, 86th, 87th, 89th, and 108th of Foot and the former 'special' unit, the Ulster Defence Regiment, which was neither a Territorial Army unit, nor a Regular Army unit, but contained part-time soldiers.

The Parachute Regiment
Formed in 1942 as part of the Army Air Corps, whose badge they wore until May 1943, when the well-known wings and parachute badge was authorised.

The Royal Gurkha Rifles
Formed in 1994 from the 2nd, 6th, 7th, and 10th Gurka Rifles. The missing numbered Gurkha units were absorbed by the Indian and Pakistani armies upon Independence in 1947.

The Rifles
Formed in 2007 from 11th, 13th, 28th, 32nd, 39th, 43rd, 46th, 49th, 51st, 52nd, 53rd, 54th, 60th, 62nd, 66th, 68th, 85th, 99th, 105th, 106th of Foot, and the Rifle Brigade.

Appendix 8

LOOKING AT PHOTOGRAPHS

When a military photo comes up for discussion on a web page, a Facebook group or at a family history event, my first question is usually, 'have you got the original?'

The original photograph can offer so much more. The prolonged exposure of late Victorian cameras lends itself well to the family regimental detective. They can be so clear that on these original prints it is not unusual to be able to read the inscription on the buttons. If these are then presented on a poor photocopy, all of this lovely detail is lost.

First of all, look closely at the badge, if visible, under a magnifying glass or 'jeweller's loupe'. In images taken before the cheaper cameras of the 1920s you should be able to make out the shape.

Compare the uniform to the chapter on dating and, if in doubt, there are other books available that go into greater detail. What I have presented herein is just a basic timeline.

Once you have put these two elements together, it is then a good idea to look on the back. Often, a photographer will either advertise on the rear (or on the front). Sometimes these are barely visible, non-coloured embossing to the photo itself in a corner.

Unless the photo has been used as a postcard – this was the cheapest option when ordering prints, hence there are so many out there – you may not find any names there. If you do, beware. A well-meaning but ill-informed family member may have scribbled a name there which could be totally wrong. Always take any writing on the rear with a pinch of salt. A chum may have written a post-war address and name there for contact details; a cribbage game may well have been scored there. There can be a myriad of reasons as to why there is something written there and not all of these point to the correct identity of the subject!

The rear may read POST CARD in large capitals. These are British produced cards. Quite often you will also see CARTE POSTALE, and these can come from anywhere from France and Belgium to even Egypt.

During the First World War, photographers saw an 'opportunity'. They would drive around the various base locations in a small lorry or car with developing tanks, a prop or two, their camera and stand, and a large painted backdrop which could be hung in any doorway, or even on the side of a barn.

These pictures are fairly easy to identify by the amount of light, the slight gap at the bottom of the backdrop, muddy boots and the carrying of respirators (gas masks) especially.

These pictures could then be sent home and distributed amongst the family.

Walking Out Canes in photographs should be treated with caution as they do not show that the man pictured was an officer. They were carried by all ranks after 1800 hours, local time – after duties – when the 'rough soldiery' were let out into the local area. Officers had officers' canes, which could be anything from a curve-handled walking stick, a leather or covered cane to a huge 'shillelagh' (pronounced shill-lay-lee) carried by some of the senior non-commissioned officers and all of the commissioned officers of the Irish regiments. The Walking Out Canes of the other ranks had silver or white metal tops decorated with the badge of the regiment. Officers did not usually carry this type. Of course, there is always an exception to any rule, and it can normally be found in a photograph, because the unusual was photographed! 'One swallow does not a summer make', as I often quote when presented by an oddity.

There were women in the forces after 1915/1916. These women though did not dress as per the men. If you see a patent woman in a photo, in what is patently a male uniform – i.e. not a dress – you can almost certainly say that that she is dressed in her husband's or boyfriend's uniform. Women in uniform were members of, for example, the QAIMNS, TFNS, the WAAC, the WRAF and the WRNS. Some WAAC (QMAAC) were rebadged as ASC as they were in the Forage Corps, or motordrivers or dealt with remounts. Photographic examples of the above can be seen in chapter 30.

One of the oft quoted sayings is that, 'he's only a poor boy, he should be at school'. More often than not, the boy in the image is at school. Many schools throughout the country had cadet units and in the grammar and public school sector, they had Officer Training Corps. These were cadet units that trained just the same as the Army Cadets do today; they attended camps, went to shooting competitions and wore military uniforms.

Another cadet unit that I have pictured, as they come up so often, is the Church Lads' Brigade, who were officially allied to the King's Royal Rifle Corps. The picture and the badge can be found on page 65.

Boys were recruited between 12 and 15 years of age to see if they had musical aptitude by both the volunteers and the regular forces during the 19th and early 20th century. If they did, they remained with the depot band until they could be posted to one of the battalions. Even in those days, 18 was the age for regular service. If they were found not to have the sufficient standard for a military band, they often became Drummer boys.

The boys' battalions, junior leaders' regiments and divisional junior bands continued well into the modern age. It was only with the reorganisations of the army in the early 1990s that most of them vanished into history. I have fond memories of the Junior Band of the Depot, Queen's Division at Bassingbourn Barracks in the 1980s.

Under 18s can still join the army today as Junior Soldiers. The Royal Navy had a similar system, as did the Royal Air Force for junior entry.

Appendix 9

REGIMENTAL AND SERVICE NUMBERS

Through the 19th century and into the First World War, and then the Second World War and beyond, recruits were not always enlisted in their local county regiments and, after 1942, with the introduction of centralised training under the badge of the General Service Corps, numbers were no longer regimentally allocated, which identified a particular regiment or corps as it did from 1920 until that date. Instead, from 1942, recruits were allocated true army (as opposed to regimental) 'service numbers', and thus, one cannot identify a soldier's cap badge using their number, only that they joined from 1942 onwards. After training, where they wore badges as General Service Corps, they were allocated to their new cap badge, which was where there were requirements at that point, along with this same training centre allocated service number.

Pre-1920
Prior to 1920, each regiment had its own system of regimental numbers, with each regiment starting at 1. If a soldier transferred to another regiment he got a new number.

1920-1942
A replacement system was introduced in 1920 under Army Order 388, and remained in place until 1942, wherein each regiment was allocated its own block of numbers, allowing the family historian to find the regiment their ancestor was in. See the list below for the blocks of numbers.

Post 1942
After 1942 it becomes a little more difficult to identify a regiment when no personal papers are traceable. One must then look at marriage certificates, the 1939 Register, photos and any birth certificates for clues.

Large numbers of men were being conscripted and sent to a central depot where they had their medicals and were allocated a number *before* being posted to a regiment. It was too much of an administrative job for the central depots to administer the old regimental numbers so a single system of army (as opposed to regimental) numbers was introduced. These numbers were allocated in blocks in the 14xxxxxx, 16xxxxxx and 19xxxxxx series. This numbering system was then rationalised into the 1950-2007 numbering system, and the subsequent post-2007 numbering system.

Officers

Officers and all officer-ranked Corps such as the Queen Alexandra's Imperial Military Nursing Service (QAIMNS) – (once they became fully fledged officers and not 'of officer status'), – were numbered differently and are not covered here.

The best place for researching an officer is via the *Army List*, and the *London Gazette*. As I have mentioned, the *Gazette Online* is a bit of a minefield, and can be a problem to navigate when looking for an individual.

1920-1942 Regimental Numbers

See below each regiment's allocated block of numbers, as follows:

- Royal Army Service Corps 1 - 294000 and 10660001 - 11000000
- The Life Guards 294001 - 304000
- Royal Horse Guards 304001 - 309000
- Cavalry of the Line 309001 - 721000 (Inclusive of 558471 to 558761 allocated to the Royal Armoured Corps, extra to the block of numbers later allocated)
- The Royal Regiment of Artillery (Field, Coastal & Anti-Aircraft) 721001 - 1842000 and 11000001 - 11500000
- Royal Engineers 1842001 - 2303000
- Royal Corps of Signals 2303001 - 2604000
- Grenadier Guards 2604001 - 2646000
- Coldstream Guards 2646001 - 2688000
- Scots Guards 2688001 - 2714000
- Irish Guards 2714001 - 2730000
- Welsh Guards 2730001 - 2744000
- The Black Watch (The Royal Highland Regiment) 2744001 - 2809000
- Seaforth Highlanders 2809001 - 2865000
- Gordon Highlanders 2865001 - 2921000
- Cameron Highlanders 2921001 - 2966000

- Argyll and Sutherland Highlanders 2966001 - 3044000
- Royal Scots 3044001 - 3122000
- Royal Scots Fusiliers 3122001 - 3178000
- The Kings Own Scottish Borderers 3178001 - 3233000
- Cameronians (Scottish Rifles) 3233001 - 3299000
- Highland Light Infantry 3299001 - 3377000
- East Lancashire Regiment 3377001 - 3433000
- Lancashire Fusiliers 3433001 - 3511000
- Manchester Regiment 3511001 - 3589000
- Border Regiment 3589001 - 3644000
- The Prince of Wales' Volunteers 3644001 - 3701000
- The King's Own Royal Regiment 3701001 - 3757000
- The King's Regiment 3757001 - 3846000
- The Loyal Regiment 3846001 - 3902000
- South Wales Borderers 3902001 - 3947000
- Welch Regiment 3947001 - 4025000
- The King's Shropshire Light Infantry 4025001 - 4070000
- Monmouthshire Regiment 4070001 - 4103000
- Herefordshire Regiment 4103001 - 4114000
- Cheshire Regiment 4114001 - 4178000
- Royal Welch Fusiliers 4178001 - 4256000
- Royal Northumberland Fusiliers 4256001 - 4334000
- East Yorkshire Regiment 4334001 - 4379000
- The Green Howards 4379001 - 4435000
- Durham Light Infantry 4435001 - 4523000
- West Yorkshire Regiment 4523001 - 4601000
- The Duke of Wellington's Regiment (The West Riding) 4601001 - 4680000
- The King's Own Yorkshire Light Infantry 4680001 - 4736000
- York & Lancaster Regiment 4736001 - 4792000
- Lincolnshire Regiment 4792001 - 4848000
- Leicestershire Regiment 4848001 - 4904000
- South Staffordshire Regiment 4904001 - 4960000
- Sherwood Foresters 4960001 - 5038000
- North Staffordshire Regiment 5038001 - 5094000
- Royal Warwickshire Regiment 5094001 - 5172000
- Gloucester Regiment 5172001 - 5239000
- Worcestershire Regiment 5239001 - 5328000
- Royal Berkshire Regiment 5328001 - 5373000
- Oxfordshire & Buckinghamshire Light Infantry 5373001 - 5429000
- The Duke of Cornwall's Light Infantry 5429001 - 5485000

- Hampshire Regiment 5485001 - 5562000
- Wiltshire Regiment 5562001 - 5608000
- Devonshire Regiment 5608001 - 5662000
- Somerset Light Infantry 5662001 - 5718000
- Dorsetshire Regiment 5718001 - 5763000
- Royal Norfolk Regiment 5763001 - 5819000
- Suffolk Regiment 5819001 - 5875000
- Northamptonshire Regiment 5875001 - 5931000
- Cambridgeshire Regiment 5931001 - 5942000
- Bedfordshire & Hertfordshire Regiment 5942001 - 5998000
- Essex Regiment 5998001 - 6076000
- The Queen's Royal Regiment 6076001 - 6132000
- East Surrey Regiment 6132001 - 6188000
- Middlesex Regiment 6188001 – 6278000
- The Buffs (East Kent Regiment) 6278001 - 6334000
- Royal West Kent Regiment 6334001 - 6390000
- Royal Sussex Regiment 6390001 - 6446000
- Royal Fusiliers 6446001 - 6515000
- The Inns of Court Regiment 6802501 - 6814000
- Honourable Artillery Company (Infantry) 6825001 - 6837000
- The King's Royal Rifle Corps 6837001 - 6905000
- The Rifle Brigade 6905001 - 6972000
- Royal Inniskilling Fusiliers 6972001 - 7006000
- Royal Ulster Rifles 7006001 - 7040000
- Royal Irish Fusiliers 7040001 - 7075000
- Royal Dublin Fusiliers 7075001 - 7109000 (Disbanded 1922)
- Royal Irish Regiment 7109001 - 7143000
- Connaught Rangers 7143001 - 7177000 (Disbanded 1922)
- Leinster Regiment 7177001 - 7211000 (Disbanded 1922)
- Royal Munster Fusiliers 7211001 - 7245000 (Disbanded 1922)
- Royal Army Medical Corps 7245001 - 7536000
- Royal Army Dental Corps 7536001 - 7539000 and 10510001 - 10530000
- Royal Guernsey Militia and Royal Alderney Artillery Militia 7539001 - 7560000 (Discontinued in 1929)
- Royal Militia of the Island of Jersey 7560001 - 7574000 (Discontinued in 1929)
- Royal Army Ordnance Corps 7574001 - 7657000 and 10530001 - 10600000.
- Royal Army Pay Corps 7657001 - 7681000 and 10400001 - 10500000. (Locally enlisted staff Middle East 10500001 - 10508000)
- Royal Military Police 7681001 - 7717000

- Military Provost Staff Corps 7717001 - 7718800
- Small Arms School Corps 7718801 - 7720400
- Royal Army Education Corps 7720401 - 7732400
- Band of the Royal Military College 7732401 - 7733000
- Corps of Military Accountants 7733001 - 7757000 (Disbanded 1925)
- Royal Army Veterinary Corps 7757001 - 7807000
- Machine Gun Corps 7807001 - 7868000 (Disbanded 1922)
- Royal Tank Regiment 7868001 - 7891868
- Royal Armoured Corps 7891869 - 8230000 also 558471 - 558761
- Militia 10000000 - 10350000 (Army Numbers were allocated in accordance with Regulations for the Militia [Other than the Supplementary Reserve], 1939, paras. 11-13)
- Intelligence Corps 10350001 - 10400000
- Reconnaissance Corps 10600001 - 10630000
- Army Catering Corps (from 1941) 10630001 - 10655000
- Army Physical Training Corps 10655001 - 10660000
- Royal Pioneer Corps 13000001 - 14000000
- The Lowland Regiment 14000001 - 14002500
- The Highland Regiment 14002501 - 14005000
- General Service Corps 14200001 - 15000000
- Indian local enlistments 15000001 - 15005000
- Royal Electrical and Mechanical Engineers 16000001 - 16100000
- Non-Combatant Corps 97000001 - 97100000
- Auxiliary Territorial Service W/1 - W/500,000
- Voluntary Aid Detachments W/500001 – W/1000000

Appendix 10

THE MISSING NUMBERS

*T*he list of current infantry regiments and their antecedent numbers
(see Appendix 7) have several missing due to a number of Irish regiments
being disbanded in 1922 after independence, and others being disbanded later. The
anomaly is the Royal Irish Regiment, which is a return of the old name on the
amalgamation of the Royal Irish Rangers and the Ulster Defence Regiment in 1992.

The Royal Irish Regiment
1684-1922
Between being raised in 1684 and the battle of Namur in 1695, the
regiment served as Marines. After Namur they were known as 'the Royal
Regiment of Foot of Ireland', due to their gallantry in front of the King.

The Cameronians (Scottish Rifles)
1689-1968
The Regiment was formed in one day, 14 May 1689, 'without beat of drum'
(regiments for many years recruited by sending a recruiting sergeant and a
drummer to beat the drum at the market cross or outside an inn to call forward
potential recruits). They mustered on the banks of the Douglas Water in
South Lanarkshire. The regiment took its name from Richard Cameron, 'the
Lion of the Covenant'. Originally a field preacher, he was killed, a bounty on
his head, at the battle of Airds Moss in 1680. Their first commanding officer,
Cleland, had led the Covenanters in battles at Drumclog and Bothwell Brig.
His sword can still be seen in the Regimental Museum in Hamilton, along
with the 'Bloody Banner' carried by the Covenanters at both battles.

The York and Lancaster Regiment
1756-1968
Raised in 1756 and served in West Indies until 1796. Upon its return, so
many men had been lost that it had to take in many Parish Boys (male
orphans) to fill the ranks.

BIBLIOGRAPHY AND FURTHER READING

Anon, *Regimental Nicknames and Traditions of the British Army*, Gale and Polden, 1915

Bowling, A.H., *British Hussar Regiments 1805 to 1914*, Almark Publishing, 1972

Brereton, J.M., *A Guide to the Regiments and Corps of the British Army*, The Bodley Head, 1985

Clabby, Brigadier J., *The History of the Royal Army Veterinary Corps 1919 to 1961*, J.A. Allen and Co, 1963

Cox, Reginald H.W., *Military Badges of the British Empire*, Ernest Benn, 1982

Cross, W.K., *The Charlton Standard Catalogue of First World War Canadian Infantry Badges*, The Charlton Press, 1991

Edwards, Major T.J., *Regimental Badges*, Gale and Polden, 1963 (ed)

Gaylor, John, *Military Badge Collecting*, Seeley Service, 1971 and editions

Hobart, Malcolm C., Badges and Uniforms of the Royal Air Force, Leo Cooper, 2000

Hodges, Lieutenant Colonel Robin, *British Army Badges*, Published by Lt Col and Mrs Hodges, 2005

Kipling, Arthur & King, Hugh, *Head-dress Badges of the British Army in Two Volumes*, Frederick Muller Ltd, 1979

Ripley, Howard, *Buttons of the British Army 1855 to 1970*, Arms and Armour Press, 1971 and reprints

Smith, Major General Sir Frederick, *A History of the Royal Army Veterinay Corps 1796 to 1919*, Balliere and Tindall and Cox, 1927

Westlake, Ray, *A Guide to the British Army's Numbered Infantry regiments 1751 to 1881*, Naval and Military Press 2018

Westlake, Ray, *A Guide to the British Home Service Helmet and its Badges 1878 to 1914*, Naval and Military Press, 2020

Westlake, Ray, *A Guide to the British Line Infantry Regiments 1881 to 1914*, Naval and Military Press, 2020

Westlake, Ray, *A Guide to the Volunteer Training Corps 1914 to 1918*, Naval and Military Press, 2020

Westlake, Ray, *A Register of the Territorial Force Cadet Units 1910 to 1922*, Naval and Military Press, 2019

Westlake, Ray, *Kitchener's Army*, Spellmount, 1989 and editions

White, Arthur S., *A Bibliography of Regimental Histories of the British Army*, The Society for Army Historical Research, 1965 & Naval and Military Press, 1992 (rpt)

Wilkinson, F., *Cavalry and Yeomanry Badges of the British Army 1914*, Arms and Armour Press, 1973

Wilkinson, F., *Badges of the British Army 1920 to the present*, Arms and Armour Press, 1997

Young, Michael, *Army Service Corps 1902 to 1918*, Leo Cooper, 2000

All regiments and some very small units published their histories. These can be anything from The Grenadier Guards 1939 to 1945 to the 12th battalion the Northamptonshire Home Guard (a very small, town centre unit). They are out there.

A large number are listed in Arthur S. White's book, A Bibliography of Regimental Histories of the British Army, but since its publication many, many more would have been added to the roll.